# INDIAN
## food

**R&R PUBLICATIONS** MARKETING PTY LTD

Published by:
R&R Publications Marketing Pty. Ltd.

ABN 78 348 105 138

12 Edward Street
Brunswick, Victoria 3056
Australia

Phone: (61 3) 9381 2199

Fax: (61 3) 9381 2689

Australia-wide toll free: 1 800 063 296

E-mail: info@randrpublications.com.au

Web: www.randrpublications.com.au


Indian food


Publisher: Richard Carroll

Production Manager: Anthony Carroll

Food Photography: Alfonso Calero

Travel Text: Kerry Kenihan

Photography of India:
Stock Photos Pty Ltd

Food Stylist: Liz Nolan

Assisting Home Economist: Jenny Fanshaw

Recipe Development: Jenny Fanshaw,
Ellen Argyriou, Janet Lodge

Creative Director: Aisling Gallagher

Computer Graphics: Elain Wei Voon Loh

Editor: Fiona Brodribb

Proofreader: LoftCom

Includes index

ISBN 1 74022 147 8

EAN 9 781740 221 474


This edition printed October 2004

Computer typeset in Gill Sans,
Humanist, Futura and Giovanni

Printed in China

# CONTENTS

# the land AND ITS PEOPLE

| | |
|---|---|
| Status | Federal Republic |
| Area | 3, 287, 00 sq km |
| Population | 1 billion |
| Language | Hindi, English, Urdu |
| Religion | Hindu, Buddhist, Muslim, Christian, Sikh, Jain |
| Currency | Rupee |
| National Day | 26 January |

## WISH UPON A MOON

The Maharani of Bobbili from southern India, on holiday in her country's north, was resplendent in a superb silk sari. She had once represented India as an opponent of Australian tennis champion, Evonne Goolagong. Garlanded with cheap baubles bought from floating vendors who had also sold us flowers and sweetmeats from their gondola-like *shikaras*. We sat on an outdoor deck of our houseboat. We were moored in darkness, facing Lake Nagin, replete after a splendid, robust Kashmiri lamb dinner. We were not far from Srinigar, Kashmir's state capital which is set on Lake Dal, and is the gateway to the fabled Vale of Kashmir, the Venice of the East.

A full moon soared above us, illuminating the snow on the high, white peaks of the Himalayas ahead. The peaks were like iridescent ice creams topping dark, tall, menacing, mysterious cones. The moon's beam crept steadily towards us across the calm lake which was reflecting the snow-capped mountains. The Maharani whispered: 'As the full moon's light across the water strikes you, make a wish to return to India – and you will.'

My wish came unexpectedly true years later. I revisited many parts of India and Kashmir. I ate, north-Indian-style, on the floors of the homes of the people who had welcomed me on my previous visits to Northern India. I spent a day exploring Srinigar's canals where the *shikara* man prepared me a Moghul-style lunch on a brazier in his little boat.

The food of Jammu and Kashmir is similar to that of its neighbouring state, Himachal Pradesh. Kulu is the nation's honeymoon capital. Here, the snows of the lower Himalayas entice newly married couples to frolic in their silken wedding finery, oblivious to cold temperatures until they shelter around fires in makeshift wooden huts, eating hot freshly cooked snacks with chai (tea).

The Indian sub-continent is the world's seventh largest country with a land area of 3, 287, 00 square kilometres (1, 261, 000 square miles). Imagine a nation almost as wide as Australia or the USA. India is a federal republic with a population of more than one billion people: the world's second largest population after China. It is surrounded by Pakistan, Afghanistan, China, Tibet, Nepal, Bhutan, Bangladesh and Burma (Myanmar). West is the Arabian Sea. South is the Indian Ocean where lies the independent island of Sri Lanka (formerly Ceylon), which shares some of southern India's food traditions. East lies the Bay of Bengal.

Including the national capital territory of Delhi and its capital New Delhi, India has six union territories and 25 states which are more diverse than the countries of Europe. The idyllic Andaman and Nicobar groups of more

than 500 islands which are also controlled by India, feature tropical rainforests, hundreds of bird species and beaches lapped by waters that scuba divers dream about.

India is a kaleidoscope of civilisations, architecture, music, dance, literature, fairs, festivals and religions, not to mention its huge variety of cuisines. The contrasts of India inspire awe in visitors to the sub-continent. India's scenery is dramatic: the dominant Himalayas descend into desert alongside, rolling plains, tropical forests and beaches washed by three seas.

The wildlife of India will stir the imagination of any reader who, as a child, was captivated by pictures of tigers, panthers, elephants and monkeys. India reveres its past – reflected in its sculptures, palaces, temples, tombs, mosques, cathedrals and memorials. and that monument to love, the Taj Mahal.

## A SOUL TO BE GLIMPSED

Travellers to India can still travel through seven cities on a royal vintage train, built more than 90 years ago for princely rulers and British viceroys and eat as royally as they did. Its possible to stay at a former British Hill station or a former Maharajah's palace. Travellers can take a stroll on a golden beach at Goa or dine in a resort restaurant which could have been plucked from a Portuguese village. Goan food was strongly influenced by the Portuguese occupation from 1510–1961.

On my own travels I have stalked tigers in Corbett National Park, ridden elephants in Rajasthan and, in a dusty village of Untouchables the caste system still exists unofficially, I joined the local women in the dust, grinding spices with mortar and pestle. Although we did not share a common language, these women shared their modest meal of dhal and rice with me. The fiery food, our laughter and my gestures of appreciation were our bonds.

*India*

# The land and
# ITS PEOPLE

In New Delhi, a party was given for me by travel agents and their wives in an affluent household. Women finished the preparation of the seemingly endless dishes, while the men drank local Indian beer and talked of politics and their nation. The children were fed first, and slept while the adults conversed I tasted everything, it seemed, that India had to offer. The food was hot, cold, savoury, sweet, sour, fresh and exciting. As a foreign guest, I was not permitted to help in the crowded kitchen.

At dawn, pilgrims, residents and gurus bathed in the mighty Ganges (also known as the Ganga or Mother of India), meditated, threw marigold garlands into the water, prepared funeral pyres and lit breakfast fires to heat their dhal and rice. The city of New Delhi, as old as Babylon, blinked in the reflections.

Hundreds of tributaries flow from the Himalayas into the Ganga. Other major Indian rivers are the Indus, which sustains India's wheat bowl, and the Punjab. East is the river Brahmaputra. Water for crops is as well as on these rivers dependent on the monsoon season.

Since ancient times, India has attracted people in search of something: often peace and religious enlightenment but sometimes war. Greece's Alexander the Great invaded India in 327 BC and, down the centuries, clans, empires, states, religious groups, sultanates and conquerors have all battled on Indian soil. In 1509, Goa was seized and made Portugal's maritime capital, and from 1616, as the English influence rose, Portugal's power was waning, the English through the East India Company. The English took control of other princely states and their spices. Colonising French traders were also lured to India by its spices.

Persians, Islamic Moghuls, Romans, Jews, Christians (according to legend, St Thomas the Apostle had been in Kerala in AD 52), Portuguese and British have all had their impact on India; their influences remain to intrigue tourists.

Visitors are often surprised that 21st century India is also modern, with world-standard facilities, more than America's share of millionaires, and with information technology second only to the USA. India's film industry, based in Mumbai (formerly known as Bombay), is the world's largest. But affluence is also sadly offset by appalling poverty.

India practises more religions than any nation on earth and many eating habits are a result of individual beliefs. Over 820 million people practise Hinduism, which is a lifestyle as well as a series of beliefs. Hindus do not eat beef because the cow is sacred to them. Buddhism was born in India but has spread so widely that every fourth human-being on earth adheres to Buddhist principles. These include vegetarianism, avoiding harm to any living thing and abstinence from alcohol. Jainism arose as a reaction to personal excesses by early Hindu priests. It does not embrace a single god, but believes in the symbiosis of all living things.. Almost a bridge between Hinduism and Islam, Sikhism emerged in the 15th century. Male devotees do not cut their hair and can be recognised by their turbans. In the 7th century, Zoroastrianism came to India from Persia and is practised by people known as Parsis, most of whom live in Mumbai. Parsis have their own vibrant food culture, a blend of Persian and Indian cuisine. Judaism came to India after the fall of Jerusalem in 587 BC. Most Indian Jews later emigrated to Israel. Although legend describes the arrival of St Thomas, it is St Bartholomew who is credited with being the first Christian missionary. St Francis Xavier came to Goa in 1542, thousands of Catholic pilgrims visit the Basilica of the Born Jesus on December 3 to view his casket. The pilgrims eat Portuguese-influenced food in celebration of his life. Protestant German, Danish and Dutch missionaries followed the Portuguese. The Christian religion was protected over two centuries under the British Raj. Arab traders brought Islam to India in the 7th century, and religious tolerance was particularly propounded by the great Moghul emperor Akbar.

In many thickly forested areas, scattered around India, 70 million people belonging to 500 tribes, collectively known as Adivasis and believed to originate from the pre-Aryan era, still live by subsistence hunting as in ancient times. But they are being gradually pressured to adopt modern methods of cultivation.

About 300 million people live in cities and towns, but agriculture remains India's most important industry, with 60 percent of the land under cultivation. Basmati rice is grown in the Himalayan foothills, where delectable fruits, including apples and apricots, also thrive. Rice is also grown in the Punjab in the north-west, but there wheat is the staple food. Breads such as naan, and tandoor (clay oven)-cooked food have come to west India from the Punjab. In the north, sheep and goats graze in cool, hilly conditions, while Bengali food in the east focuses on tropical produce, coconut, fish and mustard. Darjeeling tea, India's best-known tea, grows in the green Assam Hills.

On the south-west coast, Kerala produces 95 per cent of the republic's pepper and 60 per cent of its cardamom, on hills where there are also forests and rubber, tea and coffee plantations. Rice is so important to the diet of southern Indians, that it is celebrated early each year at the Pongal festival.

The state of Uttar Pradesh, in the east, yields more than half of India's sugarcane and grows more cereals than any other state. Sugarcane is also grown in the state of Maharashtra (whise capital is Mumbai), where cotton is produced, as well as millet, barley and peanuts. Further south, tropical Goa's main products are fish and nuts such as cashews. Rice and fish are staples of lush southern India and are served heavy with spices..

A recent survey conducted by the Indian-based Oberoi Group of Luxury Hotels reveals that Indian food has replaced roast beef in popularity in England: chicken tikka masala is now the United Kingdom's favourite dine-out dinner. Curry houses have been in existence in Britain since the 1940s, and are now an established part of British cuisine. Some people believe that Indian food always means hot curries, but, Indian cuisine may be hot, mildly cool, subtle or pungent, tempered by yoghurt and/or coconut.

The word 'curry' is derived from *kari*, a mixture of spices including cumin, coriander, turmeric, fennel, fenugreek, cloves, cinnamon and cardamom, and often garlic, with chilli the dominant spice.

Commercial curry powder was created by the British: it would never be found in India. My mother thought she was daringly different in the 1960s when she threw a teaspoon of Clive of India curry powder into a stew and served it with rice. For me as a teenager, it was a crude but exciting introduction to a wonderful and enticing cuisine.

*India*

# Daily food
# IN INDIA

## SPICE OF LIFE

Find a sparrow. Spice it. Stuff it inside a quail and then the quail into a chicken and the chicken into a sand grouse. Stuff the lot inside a peacock. Put this into a goat. Then place the goat into a camel. Dig a hole in hot sand and throw in the stuffed camel after you've lit a fire and the coals are glowing. Cover with sand and after several hours, remove the lot – this is how the royal families of India's Rajasthan once feasted in the 6th century.

India celebrates so many festivals, special religious celebrations and national days that they are too numerous to list in this context. Government of India tourism offices in your own countries will gladly inform you of festival dates (which alter annually) so that you can plan your visit to the sub-continent to coincide with them. Indians welcome foreigners to share in their religious celebations, which include the worship of cobras and elephants; of gods and goddesses; fireworks; singing; processions; music and dance; plays; fairs; and, always, festive food after fasting days have ended.

Some cookbook writers list four major cuisines of India. After several visits to India, I have discovered seven. You will find a cross-section of recipes from the seven cuisines in this book.

**North Indian:** The hearty food of the north has Muslim and Moghul influences, resulting in a variety of savoury, rich lamb and goat dishes based on cooking with ghee and cream. The cuisine was further enhanced by the tandoor method of cooking which was indigenous to the north-west frontier, now the Punjab and Pakistan. The tandoor (clay oven), which burns

wood or charcoal, imparts an unparalleled smoky flavour to mildly spiced, tender meats, lake and river fish, poultry, meat and breads. Punjabi food is simple and filling, an amalgamation of the cuisines of the Greeks, Persians, Afghans, Moghuls and northern invaders. If you see a restaurant advertising 'frontier food', it is likely to include tandoor and Punjabi food which is well worth experiencing before you create your own.

**Maharashtrian:** The people of the state of which Mumbai is the capital prepare healthy food with an emphasis on rice, vegetables (as Maharastrians people are vegetarians), nuts and nut oils. Often vegetables are spiced with a combination of ground and roasted cumin seeds, sesame seeds, cardamom, cinnamon and coconut. Sweet and sour dishes make for tantalising eating.

**Parsi:** Like Christians, the Parsis have no religious dietary restrictions. Their cuisine is not overly hot, it is a favourite with many foreigners. With Persian heritage, the Parsis are into meat, fish and eggs. If a Parsi cook needs a new idea, he/she adds eggs. Traditionally eaten on Sunday, Parsis, most resident in Mumbai, add several dhals, (lentil sauces,) to meat, chicken and meat balls (deep fried,) with caramelised brown rice.

**Gujurati:** From Maharashtra's neighbouring state of Gujurati comes an interesting vegetarian cuisine, called *thali (see page 10)*. The food is oil-free and *Thali* restaurant waiters will refill your bowls until you are fully satisfied. *Thali* has become an institution in India's major cities (see next page for more detail). It is not all vegetarian but is served with meat, fish or poultry, and rice. Gujuratis are fond of relishes and pickles.

**Sindhi:** The Sindhis migrated to India after the 1947 partition, bringing with them a new cuisine characterised by garlic, mint-flavoured chutneys, pickles and very sweet meats. Sindhi food is not necessarily vegetarian. An example is *kofta tas-me*. These are meat balls swathed in a sauce of onion, tomato, chilli, ginger, coriander and sprinkled with garam masala.

**The flavour of Bengali:** Freshwater and saltwater fish, seafood and the flavour of mustard seed dominate the Bengali diet. Fish is grilled, fried or stewed. Yoghurt is offered separately and is sometimes also used in preparation. Bengalis like lightly fried fish in a sauce Westerners would regard as curry flavoured – yet it's relatively mild. Bengalis also love sweet dishes.

**Goan:** The Christian Portuguese had a great influence on the tropical state of Goa, as did the Muslims. The use by the Portuguese of vinegar and the sour fruit of lokum and tamarind, have combined with a Christian preference for pork and a non-vegetarian-Hindu taste for lamb. Seafood, fish and fruits are bountiful. Goans also perfected the vindaloo. Try the vindaloo recipe on page 62 and milder the cashew-nut butter chicken on page 57.

**South Indian:** In the south, one finds a Brahmin cuisine, distinctive because strict South Indian Brahmins will not eat tomatoes and beetroot as they are blood-coloured. Nor will they eat garlic or onion. Recipes are based on tamarind, chilli, coconut, yellow lentils and rice. These, combined with a vegetable, make *sambar*, a staple dish eaten with *rasama*, a peppery, lentil-based consomme. These two dishes are the basis of English-inspired mulligatawny. This staple dish is usually eaten twice daily. Steamed dumplings and pancakes made from fermented ground rice and dhal have spread from Southern India throughout India. Meat and seafood are enjoyed by non-vegetarians. Some south Indian dishes can be exceedingly hot to Western palates.

### DAY BEGINS IN DARKNESS

Before dawn, millions of Indians rise to prepare breakfast. Many rush to feed the family before sunrise because they have employment and may have to travel long distances to reach it. So from 3 am, braziers are alight in the streets. The smoke haze and the aromas of spicy dhal sauces permeate the air. As the food cooks, the stallholders weave marigold garlands or sew by the light of the fire. Women are usually the cooks in India. While some women become doctors, company directors and politicians, as did one of the world's first woman prime ministers, Indira Ghandi, women usually still do the majority of houshold work in India. Marriages are still arranged and in some cases a wife will never have met her husband before the wedding.

*daily food*

# INTRODUCTION

Among the poorer classes, girls often do not go to school but clean the house and cook while their parents go to work in industry or to the fields. Children who do go to school usually eat curried dhal for breakfast in the north, or snacks. In the south children breakfast on *dosa* (curried lentils and rice), possibly with coconut which is thinned and crisped on a flat griddle. It may be stuffed with onions and potatoes and served on a banana leaf.

The best breakfast I've ever enjoyed in India comprised sautéed chicken livers with green masala paste (recipe page 15) and naan. This also makes a super brunch dish when combined with other dishes.

### THALI TIME – LUNCH

*Thali* is a tremendous innovation. People in business or busy homes call from the street or telephone their local *thali*-man to bring them lunch. He comes on bicycle with a cart or in a van and delivers a multi-course meal far superior to home-delivered pizza. Invented in Gujurat state and essentially vegetarian, the *thali* arrives in a metal can, like a small bucket, layered with plates of appetisers, vegetable and rice dishes. In recent times, poultry, meat and fish have been added in response to clients' requests. *Thali* may also include a dessert or sweetmeats. The *thali*-man picks up his shiny pots and payment on the next visit.

You can create your own *thalis* for lunch or dinner from this book. *Thali* is also eaten as a multi-course meal in homes and restaurants in India. All the diner has to specify is vegetarian or non-vegetarian *thali*. Different dishes come every day with some bread, an Indian *paneer* (light home-made cheese), pickles, chutney and yoghurt. In a *thali* restaurant, china bowls are filled with food and placed on a metal tray. *Thali* is also served on banana leaves. No cutlery is presented as Indians eat every meal with their right hand. The left hand is unhygienic. After practice with your fingers, you will soon become adept. And, if you dine with a Muslim or a Jew, be careful about ordering pork. Pork dishes at the table may be upsetting for strict Jews and Muslims, so choose an alternative meat or vegetable dish.

### EVENING DINING

A vegetarian dinner may comprise about five courses, including bread and/or rice. A meat-eater's meal might comprise of four courses, including a rice pudding. On a very special occasion up to nine dishes could be served, including rice and bread, plus dessert, pudding, cake or fruit.

Alcohol is not generally drunk in India, especially in strict Buddhist and Muslim homes. Some Sikhs may request a bottle of spirits from a visitor if they have no licence to buy or drink it. Indian wine does not have much of a reputation, but an imported rosé from Portugal or a similar region will certainly accompany a Goan meal well. Otherwise light beer, a fresh, dry white wine, lassi or mineral water is generally served at an Indian dinner party. Take flowers as gifts when visiting an Indian family.

*Kerry Kenihan*

*basic recipes*

# Ingredients, spices and HERBS

## INGREDIENTS

The magic of Indian cooking lies in the myriad of herbs and spices used. Every dish derives its unique taste from the different blending of herbs and spices.

There is a myth that Indian food is 'curry' – meat in a sloppy gravy – and is only good when it's hot and your mouth is crying for iced water! This concept of curry originated with the British, who ruled India for more than 200 years. The British invented a standard mixture of 'curry powder' – hot ground cayenne pepper, ground cinnamon, nutmeg, cloves, turmeric, ground cumin and ground coriander. However in India some of these spices are just not used together. Indian cooks make their own mixtures of various spices for different dishes. The secret of any dish is the mixture (*masala*) of spices used and the length of the cooking time. Spices and herbs should never be overcooked or they will lose their flavour.

## THE SPICES

*Asafoetida:* This is a hard block of resin which is used as an aid to digestion and to prevent flatulence. It is used mostly when cooking lentils and pulses. In India the block would be heated in a hot oven for 5 minutes and then ground to a fine powder in a mortar and pestle. In western countries it can be purchased already ground. It is used in minute quantities.

*Bay leaves* (tej patha): This spicy, aromatic but mellow-tasting leaf is used in sauces and rice dishes (*pullaos*).

*Black onion seeds* (kalaunji): These have no connection with onions but are so called because they resemble onion seeds. They are mainly used in rice dishes and with green, leafy vegetables in stir-fried dishes. Black onion seeds have a strong bitter-sweet flavour.

*Black peppercorns* (kali mirch): A pungent condiment that is used whole in chutneys. Ground black peppercorns are used mainly in yoghurt and salad dishes.

*Black salt* (Kali namak): This is a hard block of sulphurous rock which is spicy and extremely pungent. It should not be tasted or used by itself! Use black salt only when mixed with other ground, dry spices in chutneys, sauces and toppings. It can be purchased as a piece of rock which you can grind then keep in an airtight container.

*Cardamom* (elaichi): Cardamom provides a strong flavour which many Indian dishes require. It also helps digestion and is one of the spices used in *garam masala*.

*Cayenne pepper* (degi mirch): This is the ground powder of a red pepper originating from Kashmir. It is very hot and should be used in minute quantities in meat dishes and sweet chutneys. It can be used in place of peppers.

*Chillies* (mirch): These come in several varieties, but the following are four of the most commonly used:

>*Fresh red chillies:* These come in a variety of shapes and sizes. As a general rule, the smaller, narrower and darker the chilli, the greater its pungency.

>*Fresh green chillies:* These are 5–10 cm long and are rich in vitamins. They give a distinctive hot taste to food and will keep in an airtight container for 7–10 days.

>*Ground chillies:* Mainly used with fried vegetables as a topping.

>*Dried chillies:* Used in spice bags for *pullaos* and pickles.

*Cinnamon* (dalchini): This has a sweet spicy flavour. It is used whole in *pullaos*, desserts and chutneys. Ground, it is one of the spices used in garam masala, and is used in meat and chicken dishes and some desserts.

*Cloves* (laung): These have a pungent taste and aroma. Ground cloves make up one of the main spices in *garam masala* and are also used in tiny amounts in some desserts. Whole cloves are used in rich Indian dishes and chutneys.

*Coriander* (dhania): The seeds are used whole to flavour lentils and in some vegetable dishes. Ground coriander has a distinctive taste. Don't get carried away and add too much to food or it will be overpowering.

*Cumin* (jeera): This spice is used both as whole seeds and ground. The whole black seeds have a sweet herbal taste and are used in northern and Moglai dishes and in *biriyanis*. The white or green seeds are used whole or ground cumin has a gentle flavour and is used in appetisers, snacks, batters and yoghurts.

*Fennel* (saunf): Fennel seeds are similar to white cumin seeds and are used mainly in pickles, drinks and rice dishes. Fennel seeds are also used to aid digestion after eating. Ground fennel is used in meat, chicken and fish dishes and gives a tangy, almost minty bite.

*Fenugreek* (methi): The seeds, mainly used in lentil and some vegetable dishes, have a bitter taste. Ground fenugreek is used mainly in meat, chicken and fish dishes. Fenugreek leaves can be bought fresh or dried and are used as a flavouring for vegetables or as a herb. They have a bitter-sweet taste.

*Garlic* (lahsun): This is the root of a plant and is a very important ingredient in non-vegetarian dishes, some lentil dishes and chutneys.

*Garam masala:* The name means 'mixed spice' and it consists of cinnamon, cloves, cardamom, cumin, nutmeg, black peppercorns and coriander ground together. It can be bought ready-mixed in the spice section of most supermarkets or you can make your own (see page 14).

*Ginger* (adrak): Used both fresh and ground, ginger is the aromatic root of a tropical plant. Fresh ginger is a must in all Indian cooking. It has to be peeled before use. Ground ginger is used mainly as a topping with other dry spices for salads, fried vegetables, sweet dishes.

*Mango powder* (amchur): This is a brownish powder made from sun-dried green mangoes. It has a sour taste and imparts a unique flavour which is loved all over India.

*Mustard seeds* (rai): These come in three colours; black, brown and yellow. Black mustard seeds are used mainly in vegetarian sauces, to flavour yoghurt and in vegetable dishes. Brown mustard seeds are more difficult to find but are used in chutneys and toppings. Yellow mustard seeds are used in lentil and vegetable dishes with a tomato base.

*Nutmeg* (jaiphal): This spice is used in small quantities to give a subtle flavour to meat and rice dishes. It is also used in sweets and puddings.

*Paprika:* This spice is used mainly as a topping for salads.

*Poppy seeds* (khus-khus): These are used as a thickening agent in desserts and give a special texture to food.

*Saffron* (kesar): This is a very expensive spice which comes from Kashmir or Spain. It has an aromatic flavour and is used to colour desserts and rice dishes.

*Sesame seeds* (til): These are mainly used in chutneys, pickles and in some sweets.

*Turmeric* (haldi): Turmeric is an aromatic, pungent root. It is used ground in order to colour and flavour meat and vegetable dishes. Take care when using turmeric as it can stain.

## THE HERBS
*Basil* (tulsi): Indians revere the basil plant. Use the leaves for yoghurt and rice dishes and in sauces. Basil has a sweet, sharp taste.

*See below for ingredients, spices and herbs.*

coriander seeds

cinnamon sticks

dried chillies

fennel seeds

cloves

cardamon pods

*Chives:* Used in salads and herbs in vegetable dishes with other herbs, chives have a mild onion flavour.

*Coriander* (hara dhania)*:* Indian cooks use only the leaves of fresh coriander. When chopped, the leaves have an aromatic flavour and are used as a garnish, in chutneys and for sauces.

*Dill* (sowa)*:* Used in vegetable dishes, salads and some rice dishes, dill has a clean delicate flavour.

*Mint* (phudina)*:* This herb is used in salads and chutneys, and is mixed with other herbs in vegetable dishes.

## OTHER INGREDIENTS

*Caster sugar* (cheeni)*:* This is used in salads as well as in some meat and vegetable dishes.

*Coconut* (nariyal)*:* Used as flakes in lentil (*dhal*) dishes or grated in salads and some vegetable dishes.

*Ghee:* Clarified butter. Sold in cans, packets or tubs.

*Lemon juice* (nimbu ras)*:* Used in many recipes to give a tangy taste.

*Mustard oil* (rai-ka-tel)*:* This is used in small quantities in pickles.

*Palm sugar* (gur)*:* Used in chutneys and lentil (dhal) dishes.

*Sesame seed oil* (til-ka-tel)*:* Used in salads to give a nutty flavour.

*Tamarind* (imli)*:* Available as pieces or as a concentrate, tamarind is used in lentil (dhal) dishes and chutneys.

# Spices, mixes AND BLENDS

## AADOO MIRCH SPICE MIX

### Ingredients
55g fresh root ginger, grated
1 clove garlic, chopped
30g fresh chillies
$1/2$ teaspoon salt

### Method
1. Grind ginger and garlic in a blender or food processor, or use a mortar and pestle. Remove stalks from chillies and add with salt. Purée to a smooth paste, scrape into a bowl and cover tightly. Will keep for 1 week in the refrigerator.

Makes about 75g

## PANCH FORAN

### Ingredients
2 tablespoons black onion seeds
2 tablespoons anise seeds
1 tablespoon black or white mustard seeds
2 tablespoons ground fenugreek

### Method
1. Using a mortar and pestle, or a coffee grinder kept especially for the purpose, grind onion seeds, anise seeds and mustard seeds finely. Stir in fenugreek. Use as indicated in recipes.

Makes 6 tablespoons

## TANDOORI SPICE MIX

### Ingredients
1 small onion, chopped
3 cloves garlic, crushed
$2^{1/2}$ cm piece of fresh root ginger, peeled and finely chopped
1–2 green chillies, seeded and chopped
1 teaspoon coriander seeds
$1/2$ teaspoon cumin seeds
$1/2$ teaspoon red chilli powder
1 teaspoon paprika
$1/2$ teaspoon salt

### Method
1. Grind onion, garlic, ginger, chillies and seeds together, using a pestle and mortar, or a coffee grinder kept especially for the purpose. Add chilli powder, paprika and salt and mix well.

Makes about 6 tablespoons

## GARAM MASALA

### Ingredients
2 teaspoons cardamon seeds
2 teaspoons cumin seeds
2 teaspoons coriander seeds
1 teaspoon black peppercorns
1 teaspoon whole cloves
1 cinnamon stick, broken
$1/2$ nutmeg, grated

**Method**

1. Heat a heavy-based frying pan over moderate heat. Add cardamom seeds, cumin seeds, coriander seeds, peppercorns, cloves and cinnamon stick. Cook, stirring, until evenly browned. Allow to cool.

2. Using a mortar and pestle, or a coffee grinder kept especially for the purpose, grind roasted spices to a fine powder. Add nutmeg and mix well.

Makes about 4 tablespoons

## MASALA CURRY PASTE

**Ingredients**

3 tablespoons fresh root ginger, grated
1 teaspoon ground turmeric
1 teaspoon ground cloves
1 teaspoon ground cardamom
2 cloves garlic, crushed
6 tablespoons fresh coriander, chopped
6 tablespoons fresh mint, chopped
1/2 cup cider vinegar
60mL peanut oil
2 teaspoons sesame oil

**Method**

1. Place ginger, turmeric, cloves, cardamom, garlic, coriander, mint and vinegar in a blender or food processor; process until well combined.

2. Heat oils in a frying pan. Add spice mixture. Cook, stirring, until mixture boils, then remove from heat and allow to cool.

Makes about 1 cup

## MADRAS CURRY PASTE

**Ingredients**

6 tablespoons ground coriander
4 tablespoons ground cumin
1 tablespoon freshly ground black pepper
1 tablespoon ground turmeric
1 tablespoon black mustard seeds
1 tablespoon chilli powder
4 cloves garlic, crushed
1 tablespoon fresh ginger, finely grated
1/2 cup vinegar

**Method**

1. Place coriander, cumin, black pepper, tumeric, mustard seeds, chilli powder, garlic, ginger and vinegar in a food processor or blender and process to make a smooth paste. Heat oil in a frying pan over medium heat, add paste and cook, stirring constantly, for 5 minutes or until oil begins to separate from paste.

Makes about 3/4 cup

## GREEN MASALA CURRY PASTE

**Ingredients**

1 teaspoon fenugreek seeds, soaked in cold water overnight
3 cloves garlic, crushed
2 tablespoons fresh ginger, grated
12 tablespoons fresh coriander, chopped
12 tablespoons fresh mint, chopped
1/2 cup vinegar
1 teaspoon Thai fish sauce
2 teaspoons ground turmeric
1 teaspoon ground cardamom
1/4 cup sesame oil
1/2 cup vegetable oil

**Method**

1. Place soaked fenugreek seeds, garlic, ginger, coriander, mint and vinegar in a food processor or blender and process to make a smooth paste. Add fish sauce, turmeric and cardamom and process to combine.

2. Heat sesame and vegetable oils together in a saucepan over a medium heat for 5 minutes or until hot, stir in paste and cook, stirring constantly, for 5 minutes or until mixture boils and thickens.

Makes about 1/2 cup

## VINDALOO PASTE

**Ingredients**

1 tablespoon coriander seeds
1 teaspoon cumin seeds
1 teaspoon mustard seeds
1 teaspoon ground turmeric
1 teaspoon hot chilli powder
1 1/2 teaspoons ground ginger
pinch ground fenugreek
1 1/2 teaspoons finely ground black pepper
1 tablespoon white wine vinegar, plus extra to serve

**Method**

1. Using a mortar and pestle, or a coffee grinder kept especially for the purpose, grind whole seeds finely. Add remaining ground spices.

2. Gradually stir in vinegar to make a thick smooth paste. Store in an airtight container and moisten with an additional teaspoon of vinegar just before use.

Makes about 4 tablespoons

**Note: Leftover pastes may be stored in sterile airtight containers in the refrigerator for 8–10 days.**

# Sauces, chutneys and SAMBALS

## SPICY TOMATO SAUCE

### Ingredients

1 tablespoon oil
1 onion, chopped
1 clove garlic, crushed
2 tablespoons fresh root ginger, grated
1–2 red chillies, seeded and chopped
1 teaspoon ground turmeric
1 tablespoon ground coriander
$1/2$ teaspoon cayenne pepper
2 teaspoons paprika
2 × 400g cans chopped tomatoes
1 teaspoon each of sugar and salt
4cm slice creamed coconut

### Method

1. Heat oil in a saucepan. Fry onion, garlic, ginger and chillies until onion is golden brown. Stir in remaining spices. Cook for 2 minutes, then add tomatoes, sugar and salt. Bring to the boil, lower the heat and simmer for 20 minutes. Stir in creamed coconut until dissolved; simmer for 20 minutes more. Serve hot, with rice, dhal or naan.

Serves 4–6

## RAITA

### Ingredients

200mL natural low-fat yoghurt
salt and freshly ground black pepper, to taste
1 small onion, very finely chopped (optional)
2 tablespoons chopped fresh mint or coriander
paprika for dusting

### Method

1. In a bowl, beat yoghurt with salt and pepper. Stir in onion (if using) and add mint or coriander. Cover and chill for at least 30 minutes before serving, dusted with paprika.

Serves 4

## SPINACH RAITA

### Ingredients

1 bunch English spinach
1 cup natural yoghurt
pinch of salt
pinch of freshly ground black pepper
pinch of paprika
pinch of mango powder
2 small fresh red or green chillies, chopped

### Method

1. Steam or microwave spinach until soft. Drain, squeezing to remove excess liquid. Place spinach in a food processor or blender and purée.

2. Place yoghurt in a bowl and beat until smooth. Stir in salt, black pepper, paprika, mango powder, chillies and spinach and mix to combine.

Makes 1 cup

## SPICED YOGHURT

### Ingredients

2 cups natural yogurt
$1/2$ teaspoon freshly ground fennel seeds
salt to taste
$1/2$ teaspoon sugar
4 tablespoons vegetable oil
1 dried red chilli
$1/4$ teaspoon mustard seeds
$1/4$ teaspoon cumin seeds
4–6 curry leaves
pinch each of asafoetida and turmeric

### Method

1. In a heatproof serving dish, mix together yoghurt, fennel, salt and sugar and chill until nearly ready to serve.

2. Heat oil in a frying pan and fry chilli, mustard and cumin seeds, curry leaves, asafoetida and turmeric. When chilli turns dark, pour oil and spices over the yoghurt. Fold yoghurt mixture at the table before serving.

Serves 4

# ROASTED RED CAPSICUM RAITA

## Ingredients

2 red capsicums
2 teaspoons cumin seeds
200g tub Greek yoghurt
2 tablespoons finely chopped fresh mint
salt and black pepper to taste
1 teaspoon paprika to garnish

## Method

1. Preheat grill to high. Cut capsicums lengthways into quarters, then remove seeds, and grill them, skin-side-up, for 10 minutes or until blackened and blistered. Place in a plastic bag and leave to cool for 10 minutes.

2. Meanwhile, heat a wok and dry-fry cumin seeds over high heat for 30 seconds, stirring constantly, or until they start to pop. Remove skins from grilled capsicums and discard, then roughly chop their flesh.

3. Mix capsicums with yoghurt, cumin seeds and mint and season with salt and pepper. Transfer to a serving dish and garnish with paprika.

Serves 4

## CORIANDER AND MINT CHUTNEY

### Ingredients

3 bunches fresh coriander,
    leaves only
1 bunch fresh mint,
    leaves only
6–8 fresh green chillies
3 teaspoons fresh ginger, finely chopped
6 cloves garlic, finely chopped
2 tablespoons lemon juice
1 tablespoon caster sugar
1/4 cup water
salt to taste

### Method

1. Place coriander leaves, mint leaves, chillies, ginger, garlic, lemon juice, sugar, water and salt in a food processor or blender and process to a paste.

2. Spoon chutney into a sterilised jar, cover and refrigerate until ready to use.

Makes 2 cups

## FRUIT CHUTNEY

(opposite middle)

### Ingredients

125g dried peaches, chopped
125g dried apricots, chopped
500g Granny Smith apples, cored,
    peeled and chopped
2 teaspoons fresh ginger, finely chopped
100g sultanas
2 cups white vinegar
2 teaspoons salt
400g caster sugar
5 cloves garlic, finely chopped
3/4 teaspoon cayenne pepper (optional)

### Method

1. Place peaches, apricots, apples, ginger, sultanas, vinegar, salt, sugar, garlic and cayenne pepper (if using) in a large heavy-based saucepan. Cover and cook over a low heat, stirring occasionally, for 1 1/2 hours or until mixture is soft and pulpy.

2. Spoon chutney into hot sterilised jars. When cold, cover and label. Store in the refrigerator.

Makes 1 1/2 Litres

## LIME PICKLE

### Ingredients

20 small yellow limes
2 tablespoons salt
1 tablespoon hot chilli powder
2 tablespoons sugar
1 tablespoon black peppercorns

### Method

1. Wash limes and dry thoroughly on paper towels. Keeping each lime attached at the stalk end, cut into quarters so that can be opened up like a flower. Mix salt and chilli powder together and stuff mixture into slits in limes.

2. Pack limes into a large clean jar, sprinkling sugar and peppercorns over each layer. Cover jar with muslin; mature in a sunny place for 10–15 days.

3. To serve, separate limes into wedges and arrange in a small dish.

*Note:* This is a very hot pickle, so treat it with caution.

Makes 2 Litres

## MINT AND TOMATO CHUTNEY

(opposite, bottom)

### Ingredients

4 large tomatoes, diced
1 bunch fresh mint, leaves removed
    and coarsely chopped
1/2 cup brown sugar
1 cinnamon stick
2 bay leaves
1 teaspoon mixed spice
2 teaspoons fresh ginger, finely chopped
2 fresh red or green chillies, chopped
1/4 cup white wine vinegar

### Method

1. Place tomatoes, mint, sugar, cinnamon stick, bay leaves, mixed spice, ginger, chillies and vinegar in a heavy-based saucepan and cook over a low heat, stirring every 5 minutes, for 45 minutes or until mixture reduces and thickens.

2. Spoon chutney into a warm sterilised jar, cover and label when cold.

3. Place all ingredients in a large microwave-safe container, cover and cook on HIGH (100%) for 15 minutes. Stir and cook on MEDIUM (70%) for 15 minutes longer.

Makes 1 Litre

## MANGO CHUTNEY

(below, top)

### Ingredients

250g raisins

2 x 400g cans mangoes, drained
and cut into cubes, or 4 ripe mangoes,
peeled and cut into cubes

1 1/2 tablespoons fresh ginger, finely chopped

2 cloves garlic, finely chopped

3 teaspoons paprika

1 cinnamon stick

4 cloves

2 bay leaves

1/2 teaspoon mixed spice

3 tablespoons sultanas

1/4 cup cider vinegar

1–1 1/2 cups brown sugar

### Method

1. Place raisins in a small bowl, cover with warm water and set aside to soak for 30 minutes. Drain.

2. Place mangoes, ginger, garlic, paprika, cinnamon stick, cloves, bay leaves, mixed spice, sultanas, vinegar, sugar and raisins in a large heavy-based saucepan. Cover and cook over a low heat, stirring occasionally, for 1 hour or until chutney is thick.

3. Spoon chutney into a warm sterilised jar. Cover and label when cold. Store in refrigerator.

Makes 1 1/2 Litres

## RED CHILLI CHUTNEY

### Ingredients

10–12 fresh red chillies

10–12 cloves garlic

pinch of caster sugar (optional)

salt, to taste

water

### Method

1. Place chillies, garlic, sugar (if using) and salt in a food processor or blender and process until chopped. With machine running, add enough water to form a paste. Store in refrigerator in an airtight container.

Makes 2 cups jar

## SESAME SEED CHUTNEY

### Ingredients

1/2 cup sesame seeds

1 bunch fresh coriander, leaves only

1 bunch fresh mint, leaves only

5 fresh green chillies

1/4 cup tamarind concentrate

6–7 tablespoons water

1/2 teaspoon salt

### Method

1. Place sesame seeds in a cast-iron frying pan and dry-fry over low heat until dark brown in colour. Place sesame seeds in a food processor or blender and process until ground. Add coriander leaves, mint leaves, chillies, tamarind concentrate, water and salt, and process to make a smooth paste. Spoon chutney into a sterilised jar, cover and label. Store in the refrigerator.

Makes 2 cups

## TOMATO AND ONION SAMBAL

### Ingredients

3 large tomatoes

1 onion

3–4 spring onions

2 sprigs fresh coriander

3 tablespoons lemon or lime juice

salt and freshly ground black pepper to taste

### Method

1. Chop tomatoes, onion, spring onions and fresh coriander finely. Place in a small bowl, pour over the citrus juice and add plenty of salt and pepper to taste. Toss well, cover and set aside for 1 hour at room temperature, to allow the flavours to blend before serving.

Serves 6

## BANANA SAMBAL

### Ingredients

2 bananas

1 tablespoon lime juice

### Method

1. Slice bananas into a small bowl. Add lemon juice and toss lightly. Serve immediately.

Serves 4

## COCONUT SAMBAL

### Ingredients

55g desiccated coconut

1 tablespoon onion, finely chopped

1 small red chilli, seeded and chopped

1 tablespoon lime juice

### Method

1. Mix coconut, onion and chilli in a small bowl. Add lime juice, toss lightly and serve.

Serves 4

# snacks & appetisers

# Tasty tidbits, stunning STARTERS

Everywhere in India, you can smell and hear food sizzling, simmering and baking. Indians may be the world's greatest snackers. In restaurants and homes, snacks are before lunch or dinner. Many people enjoy common starters like these for breakfast but, inevitably, most tidbits are eaten on the run or while relaxing by the sea or in a cinema.

Samosas, with or without meat, are India's most famous snack. These, along with bhajis, pakoras, fritters and more, are usually served with sambals, bland or spicy yoghurt raita, chutneys (see page 16) and/or dhal.

Dhal is a national staple. It literally translates as 'split pea' but refers to all pulses. Dhal can be eaten as an appetiser or, as our recipes show, served over rice or with bread to make a complete meal. It is the total daily sustenance for millions of Indians. Dried peas should be soaked overnight before cooking but lentils and other pulses need less softening time. Our recipes make delicious entrees and ideal finger food for parties. Easy to prepare, these dishes are best served immediately after cooking.

## VEGETABLE BHAJIS

### Ingredients
10 shallots, finely chopped
2 zucchinis, coarsely grated
1 eggplant, finely diced
vegetable oil for frying

### Batter:
100g chickpea flour
55g ground rice
¼ teaspoon bicarbonate of soda
1 teaspoon chilli powder
1 teaspoon turmeric
1–2 tablespoons curry powder
  (mild or hot according to taste)
1 teaspoon salt
1 cup water

### Method
1. To make batter, put all ingredients into a bowl, then gradually add water, stirring constantly until combined. Add shallots, zucchinis and eggplant to batter, mixing well.

2. Pour oil into a wok to a depth of 5cm and heat over medium to high heat. Check oil is hot enough by dropping in a small piece of vegetable; it should sizzle. Gently place 4 balls of mixture (about 2 tablespoons each) into hot oil and fry for 2–3 minutes, until golden. Turn over and cook for a further 2–3 minutes, until crisp.

3. Remove bhajis with a slotted spoon and drain on kitchen towels. Fry remaining bhajis in the same way.

Serves 4

# INDIAN LENTIL SOUP (DHAL SHORVA )

## Ingredients

2 tablespoons ghee or vegetable oil

350g red lentils

1 teaspoon mustard seeds

1 teaspoon ground coriander

1 teaspoon ground cumin

1 1/2 teaspoons turmeric

1 cinnamon stick

6 cloves garlic, minced

1 tablespoon root ginger, minced

10 fresh curry leaves, bruised and tied together

1 large onion, finely chopped

1 large green chilli, whole but split

8 cups rich vegetable stock

2 tomatoes, finely diced

1 small eggplant, finely diced

1 small carrot, finely diced

1 large potato, peeled and diced

juice of 4 lemons

salt, to taste

1 bunch fresh coriander

4 tablespoons yoghurt

## Method

1.  In a large saucepan, heat ghee and add lentils, mustard seeds, coriander, cumin, turmeric, cinnamon stick, garlic, ginger, curry leaves, onion and green chilli. Cook over low heat for 5 minutes until spices are aromatic and deep brown in colour and the onion has softened.

2.  Add vegetable stock and simmer until lentils are soft; about 30–45 minutes.

3.  Remove cinnamon stick, whole green chilli and curry leaves.

4.  Blend with a hand-held mixer or food processor until smooth, then return it to the saucepan.

5.  Add diced vegetables and simmer for a further 20 minutes or until vegetables are soft.

6   Add lemon juice, salt and chopped coriander. Stir well and serve with a dollop of yoghurt, garnished with a few extra coriander leaves.

Serves 8

## SPLIT LENTIL DHAL WITH GINGER AND CORIANDER

### Ingredients

200g dried split red lentils

3$^1/_2$ cups water

$^1/_2$ teaspoon turmeric

1 tablespoon vegetable oil

1cm piece fresh root ginger, finely chopped

1 teaspoon cumin seeds

1 teaspoon ground coriander

salt and ground black pepper

4 tablespoons chopped fresh coriander, plus extra leaves to garnish

$^1/_2$ teaspoon paprika to garnish

### Method

1. Rinse lentils and drain well, then place in a large saucepan with water. Bring to the boil, skimming off any scum, then stir in turmeric. Reduce heat and partly cover pan. Simmer for 30–35 minutes, until thickened, stirring occasionally.

2. Heat oil in a small frying pan, then add ginger and cumin seeds and fry for 30 seconds or until cumin seeds start to pop. Stir in ground coriander and fry for 1 minute.

3. Season lentils with plenty of salt and pepper, then add toasted spices. Stir in chopped coriander, mixing well. Transfer to a serving dish and garnish with paprika and coriander leaves.

Serves 4

## CRUNCHY SPLIT PEAS

### Ingredients

85g yellow split peas
85g green split peas
2 teaspoons bicarbonate of soda
oil for deep-frying
$1/2$ teaspoon chilli powder
$1/2$ teaspoon ground coriander
pinch of ground cinnamon
pinch of ground cloves
1 teaspoon salt

### Method

1. Place split peas in a large bowl, cover with water, stir in bicarbonate of soda and set aside to soak overnight.

2. Rinse split peas under cold running water and drain thoroughly. Set aside for at least 30 minutes, then spread out on absorbent kitchen paper to dry. Heat about 5cm oil in a frying pan and cook split peas in batches until golden. Using a slotted spoon, remove peas and drain on absorbent kitchen paper.

3. Transfer cooked peas to a dish, sprinkle with chilli powder, coriander, cinnamon, cloves and salt and toss to coat. Allow peas to cool and store in an airtight container.

Serves 4

## SAMOSAS

(opposite)

### Ingredients

250g plain flour
$^1/_2$ teaspoon salt
30g butter
4–6 tablespoons water

### Filling:

30g butter
1 onion, finely chopped
2 cloves garlic, crushed
2 green chillies, seeded and chopped
$2^1/_2$ cm piece of fresh root ginger, grated
$^1/_2$ teaspoon ground turmeric
$^1/_2$ teaspoon hot chilli powder
370g lean minced beef or lamb
1 teaspoon salt
2 teaspoon garam masala (page 14)
juice of $^1/_2$ lemon
oil for deep-frying

### Method

1. Sift flour and salt into a bowl. Rub in butter, then mix in enough water to form a pliable dough. Knead for 10 minutes, then set aside.

2. Make filling. Melt butter in a frying pan. Add onion, garlic, chillies and ginger and fry for 5–7 minutes until onion is golden.

3. Stir in turmeric and chilli powder, then add meat and salt. Fry, stirring, until meat is cooked and mixture is fairly dry. Stir in garam masala and lemon juice; cook for 5 minutes more. Remove pan from heat and allow to cool.

4. Divide dough into 15 balls. Flatten each ball and roll out to a paper-thin circle about 10cm in diameter. Dampen edges of each circle with water and shape into cones. Fill each cone with filling, then pinch opening to seal securely.

5. Deep-fry samosas in batches in hot oil for 2–3 minutes or until golden brown. Drain on paper towels and serve.

Makes 30

### Filling Variation:

1. For a vegetarian samosa filling, fry 1 small chopped onion and 1 teaspoon grated fresh root ginger in 1 tablespoon ghee or vegetable oil until soft.

2. Stir in 370g cold mashed potato, 2 teaspoons garam masala and 1 tablespoon mango chutney (with any large chunks finely chopped.) Cook over moderate heat until mixture is fairly dry, then cool.

## TANDOORI PRAWNS

### Ingredients

18 uncooked tiger prawns, peeled and deveined, tails intact
12 spring onions, trimmed and cut into 4cm lengths
2 tablespoons coriander, finely chopped
2 tablespoons Tandoori spice mix (page 14)
1 cup natural low fat yoghurt
2 green capsicums, seeded and cut into 4cm squares
1 tablespoon oil

### Method

1. Rinse prawns and pat dry with paper towels. Place in a glass or china dish along with spring onions.

2. Stir fresh coriander and spice mix into yoghurt then add to dish. Toss spring onions and prawns in spiced yoghurt until coated. Cover dish and marinate in refrigerator for 2 hours.

3. Thread prawns, spring onions and capsicums onto kebab skewers. Stir oil into remaining marinade.

4. Cook prawn kebabs under a moderately hot grill or over medium-hot coals 6–8 minutes, turning frequently and basting with marinade. Serve immediately.

Note: If preferred, the prawns may be left in their shells, in which case the marinating time should be increased to 8 hours or overnight.

Serves 6

# samosas

## INDIAN DHAL

### Ingredients

250g brown or red lentils

4 cups water

1 teaspoon ground turmeric

1 clove garlic, crushed

30g ghee or clarified butter

1 large onion, chopped

1 teaspoon garam masala

1/2 teaspoon ground ginger

1 teaspoon ground coriander

1/2 teaspoon cayenne pepper

### Method

1. Wash lentils in cold water.

2. Place lentils, water, turmeric and garlic in a large saucepan and bring to simmering point. Cover and simmer, stirring occasionally, for 30 minutes or until lentils are cooked. Remove cover from pan, bring to the boil and boil to reduce excess liquid.

3. Melt ghee or butter in a large frying pan, add onion and cook for 5 minutes or until onion is soft. Stir in garam masala, ginger, coriander and cayenne pepper and cook for 1 minute. Stir spice mixture into lentils and serve immediately.

Serves 6

*soups*

# Warm up or
# COOL DOWN

Until recently in India, soup was not regarded as a course except in the northern snow-clad mountains or in the cold, wind-whipped, wintry deserts and plains. There, spicy and hearty soup can constitute a whole meal. A cup of hot northern soup can also be a replacement for tea to accompany other body and soul-warming dishes.

The winds of change in India and intense interest in its food from abroad has meant that the trend to serve soup in other regions is increasing. In areas of intense heat, while remaining spicy, soups are served cold. They can feature yoghurt appealing green and tropical vegetables and/or fruit including coconut, or herbs such as palate-cooling mint. Cold soup makes a refreshing summer meal starter, particularly if served with an ice cube in each bowl.

The state of Tamil Nadu, along with its warm southern state neighbours, has always favored pepper water, milagutannir, to accompany hot dishes. During the British Raj, this was adapted to become mulligatawny (recipe below). This soup, reduced in an uncovered pot till it is very thick, can be poured over rice for a very nourishing casual meal.

## MULLIGATAWNY SOUP

### Ingredients
1 tablespoon vegetable oil
2 onions, chopped
1 green apple, cored, peeled and chopped
1 clove garlic, crushed
2 tablespoons lemon juice
1 tablespoon curry powder
1 teaspoon brown sugar
1/2 teaspoon ground cumin
1/4 teaspoon ground coriander
2 tablespoons plain flour
8 cups chicken stock
500g boneless chicken breast or
    thigh fillets, cut into 1cm cubes
1/3 cup rice
freshly ground black pepper

### Method
1. Heat oil in a large saucepan over medium heat, add onions, apple and garlic and cook, stirring, for 5 minutes or until onions are tender. Add lemon juice, curry powder, sugar, cumin and coriander and cook over low heat, stirring, for 10 minutes or until fragrant.

2. Blend flour with a little stock and stir into curry mixture. Add chicken, rice and remaining stock to pan, bring to the boil, stirring constantly. Reduce heat, cover and simmer for 20 minutes or until chicken and rice are cooked. Season taste with black pepper.

*Note:* A dash of chilli sauce and a chopped tomato are delicious additions to this soup. Serve with crusty bread rolls, naan or pita bread.

Serves 4

# INDIAN SPICED POTATO AND ONION SOUP

## Ingredients

1 tablespoon vegetable oil
1 onion, finely chopped
1cm piece fresh root ginger, finely chopped
2 large potatoes, cut into 1cm cubes
2 teaspoons ground cumin
2 teaspoons ground coriander
1/2 teaspoon turmeric
1 teaspoon ground cinnamon
4 cups chicken stock
salt and black pepper
1 tablespoon natural yoghurt to garnish

## Method

1. Heat oil in a large saucepan. Fry onion and ginger for 5 minutes or until softened. Add potatoes and fry for another minute, stirring often.

2. Mix cumin, coriander, turmeric and cinnamon with 2 tablespoons of cold water to make a paste. Add to onion and potato, stirring well, and fry for 1 minute to release the flavours.

3. Add stock and season to taste. Bring to the boil, then reduce heat, cover and simmer for 30 minutes or until potato is tender. Blend until smooth in a food processor or press through a metal sieve. Return to pan and gently heat through. Garnish with yoghurt and more black pepper.

Serves 4

## COOL CUMIN-SCENTED YOGHURT SOUP

### Ingredients

1 teaspoon cumin seeds

1 teaspoon black onion seeds

1 tablespoon ghee or butter

4 spring onions, finely sliced

10 fresh mint leaves

2 teaspoons ground cumin

1 teaspoon turmeric

55g cashew nuts

310g can chickpeas, drained and rinsed

500g plain low-fat yoghurt

200mL sour cream

200mL water

salt and pepper to taste

625g cucumbers

1 tablespoon sugar

2 tablespoons shredded coconut, toasted

mint leaves and black onion seeds for garnish

### Method

1. Heat a frypan (no oil) then add cumin seeds and black onion seeds. Toss them around hot pan until the seeds smell roasted and seem to pop around the pan, about 3 minutes. Remove seeds and set aside.

2. Add the ghee to pan and add the spring onions and mint leaves and sauté for a few minutes until spring onions have wilted. Add cumin, turmeric and cashew nuts and toss until spices are fragrant and the nuts are golden. Add drained chickpeas and cook for a further 2 minutes. Set aside.

3. In a mixing bowl, whisk together yoghurt, sour cream and water until smooth. Season with salt and pepper. Peel cucumbers and scrape out seeds. Cut cucumber flesh into thin slices and add to yoghurt mixture.

4. Add spring onion and spice mixture, along with sugar, to yoghurt mixture and stir thoroughly to combine. Allow flavours to blend for 1 hour before serving.

5. Garnish with toasted coconut, sliced mint leaves and a few black onion seeds.

Serves 6

# bread & rice

# From Pilau
## TO POORI

Rice and bread are the mainstays of almost all Indian meals. Rice has been cultivated in India for more than 3,000 years and for the majority of India's 1 billion people, rice is vital for life. Plain boiled rice provides the bland contrast and balance that the palate and digestive system need to thoroughly appreciate (and tolerate) the tantalising tastes of fiery toppings.

In most Western homes, rice is served as an accompaniment to meat, poultry, fish and vegetables. In India, it is the reverse. Sometimes Western visitors to India think they are being short-changed when large amounts of rice are piled onto their plates with only a small amount of savoury dish to crown it. This is the practice even in the wealthiest of Indian households.

Basmati, a long-grained, fragrant rice, grown in the Himalayan foothills, is most used in pilaus and biryanis. It is more absorbent than short-grain rice, which is more suitable for desserts. Red rice is eaten in the rural south which has geographical conditions and a climate more conducive to rice rearing than the wheat-cultivating north; Northerners never miss their daily bread.

Indians enjoy crunchy chapatis or pappadams with each meal. Among the poor or those with religious dietary restrictions. alternatively used, the only companion to chapatis may be dhal, which may be eaten with rice. Wholemeal rice (or Indian atta) and plain flour or semolina, are to produce leavened and unleavened breads by shallow- or deep-frying, or baking. Perhaps no bread is more tempting than warm, soft naan. Traditionally baked in a tandoor (clay oven), naan is especially more-ish when served with tandoori chicken (see page 52). As few Indians have tandoors, naan is not made in the home.

Garlic naan is a favourite with Western diners. Simply add finely chopped and sauté garlic to your taste to the following plain naan recipe. Puffy pooris are proudly served on festive occasions, especially weddings.

## SPICED RICE

### Ingredients
1 1/2 cups basmati rice
4 cups water
1/2 teaspoon salt
2 tablespoons lemon juice
2 tablespoons ghee
1 medium red onion, chopped
3 tablespoons cashew nuts
3 tablespoons sultanas
1/4 teaspoon fennel seeds
1/4 teaspoon cumin seeds
1/4 teaspoon white mustard seeds
1/4 teaspoon ground turmeric
1 teaspoon ghee, extra

### Method
1. Rinse rice well in a sieve under running water. Bring 4 cups of water to boil, add salt and lemon juice. Stir in rice and, when water returns to the boil, turn down heat and simmer for 18 minutes, until rice is just tender. Drain in colander and rinse with hot water. Set aside.

2. Heat ghee in a large frying pan. Add onion and cook until transparent. Add cashews and sultanas and sauté briefly. Add spices and extra teaspoon of ghee and cook, stirring constantly, for 2 minutes.

3. Add drained rice, gently toss to combine ingredients and reheat rice. Serve hot with curries or serve as a side dish with grilled meats and chicken.

Serves 4

# FRAGRANT PILAU RICE

## Ingredients

large pinch of saffron strands
250g basmati rice
30g butter
1 shallot, finely chopped
3 cardamom pods
1 cinnamon stick
300mL water
salt to taste

## Method

1. Briefly grind saffron using a pestle and mortar, then mix powder with 1 tablespoon of boiling water and set aside. Rinse rice and drain.

2. Melt butter in a large, heavy-based saucepan. Fry shallot gently for 2 minutes or until softened. Add cardamom pods, cinnamon and rice and mix well.

3. Add water, saffron mixture and salt. Bring to the boil, then reduce heat and cover pan tightly. Simmer rice for 15 minutes or until liquid has been absorbed and the rice is tender. Remove cardamom pods and cinnamon stick before serving.

Serves 4

## COCONUT POORI

### Ingredients

200g wholemeal flour (or Indian atta flour)

100g plain flour

$1/2 - 1$ teaspoon salt

100g desiccated coconut

1 teaspoon chilli powder

$1/2$ tablespoon sugar

2 tablespoons ghee
   or vegetable oil

approximately 150mL water,

oil for frying

### Method

1. Mix wholemeal flour, plain flour, salt and coconut in a bowl with chilli powder and sugar. Add melted ghee or oil and rub through until flour appears crumbly. Stir in the water, only add water as much as necessary to form a soft dough. Knead dough well. Allow the dough to rest for 10 minutes.

2. Divide the dough into 14 pieces, flattening each and rolling each out to a thin circle of 8cm diameter.

3. Heat oil in a wok and, when hot, add one circle of dough. With a heat-proof implement, push dough under oil until dough is puffed and golden. Allow it to float, turning to cook the other side.

4. Drain on absorbent paper and cook remaining poori the same way.

*Note:* Although it is important not to overcrowd the wok, 3–4 poori can usually be cooked together.

Makes 14 poori

## NAAN BREAD

### Ingredients

1 cup plain full-fat yoghurt

1½ cups boiling water

2 cups plain flour

3 cups stoneground wholemeal plain flour

1 tablespoon yeast

2 teaspoons salt

1 teaspoon sugar

2 tablespoons nut oil (peanut or walnut
   work well)

3 tablespoons black sesame seeds

6 tablespoons sesame seeds

### Method

1. First, mix yoghurt with boiling water
   and stir well. Set aside for 5 minutes.

2. Mix plain flour with 1 cup of wholemeal flour and add
   yeast. Add yoghurt mixture and stir with a wooden
   spoon for 3 minutes, then cover with plastic wrap. Allow
   this 'sponge' to rest for 1 hour.

3. Add salt, sugar, oil and black sesame seeds and enough
   of the remaining flour to form a firm but moist dough.
   Begin to knead on a floured surface and continue until
   dough is very silky and elastic. Allow dough to rise in an
   oiled bowl for 1 hour at room temperature or until
   doubled in size.

4. Punch down dough and divide into 8 pieces. Shape each
   into a ball then flatten each piece of dough into a circle
   about 1cm thick. Transfer to oiled oven trays.

5. Brush surface of dough with water and sprinkle surface
   generously with sesame seeds. With a blade or sharp
   knife, score dough from centre to edge to look like sunrays.

6. Cover dough and allow to rise for 10 minutes. Bake on
   oiled oven trays at 230°C for 5–8 minutes.

Serves 4

## INDIAN FRESH CORN BREAD

### Ingredients

250g fresh corn kernels

1/2 teaspoon salt

2 tablespoons minced coriander

145g plain flour, plus extra for dusting

1–2 tablespoons ghee, melted

### Method

1. In a blender or food processor, grind corn and salt together until it is finely puréed.

2. Transfer mixture to a mixing bowl and add coriander. Add flour, a little at a time, continuing until mixture is kneadable (it should be a little tacky.)

3. Divide dough into 12 pieces then roll each piece out into a circle about 15cm in diameter. If dough circles are tacky, use extra flour to absorb dough moisture. Once rolled, brush each with a little ghee.

4. Heat a griddle or frying pan and add a little ghee. Add one piece of dough and cook until piece of dough underside is spotted with brown. Turn over and cook other side. Remove cooked bread and keep warm in foil while cooking other breads the same way.

*Note:* If you would like to duplicate the smoky roasted flavour that these breads would have when cooked over an open fire, simply hold each bread over a gas cooktop flame for a few seconds. Do not allow to burn. Brush with more ghee and serve.

Serves 4

## POTATO NAAN

### Ingredients

*Dough:*

1 cup plain full-fat yoghurt

1 1/2 cups boiling water

2 cups plain flour

3 cups stoneground wholemeal flour

1 tablespoon yeast

2 teaspoons salt

1 teaspoon sugar

2 tablespoons peanut oil

3 tablespoons black sesame seeds

1 egg, beaten

*Filling:*

500g potatoes, peeled and diced

1 onion, finely diced

4 mint leaves, finely sliced

1/4 cup parsley, chopped

1/2 cup coriander leaves, chopped

1/4 teaspoon cumin

1/4 teaspoon turmeric

salt and pepper, to taste

### Method

1. First, mix yoghurt with boiling water and stir well. Set aside for 5 minutes.

2. Mix plain flour with 1 cup of wholemeal flour and add yeast. Add yoghurt mixture and stir with a wooden spoon for 3 minutes then allow to rest for 30 minutes.

3. Add salt, sugar, oil and black sesame seeds and enough of the remaining flour to form a firm but moist dough.

4. Begin to knead on a floured surface and continue until dough is very silky and elastic. Allow dough to rest in an oiled bowl for 1 hour or until doubled in size.

5. Meanwhile make potato filling. Cover potatoes, and boil until soft. Mix hot potato with onion, mint leaves, parsley, coriander, cumin, turmeric and salt and pepper and mash until soft but not sloppy. Cool.

6. Punch down dough and divide into 12 equal pieces. Roll each piece into a circle about 15cm in diameter. Place a large tablespoon of filling in the centre of each dough circle and lift both edges of circle to seal. Pinch seam together very well. Allow to rise for 10 minutes then brush with beaten egg and sprinkle with sesame seeds. Bake at 200°C for 15–20 minutes or until golden and crisp.

Serves 4

## CHAPATIS

### Ingredients

250g wholemeal flour
1 teaspoon salt
1 cup water

### Method

1. Sift flour and salt into a bowl. Make a well in the centre and add water, a little at a time, using your fingers to incorporate the surrounding flour to make a smooth, pliable dough.

2. Knead dough on a lightly floured surface for 5–10 minutes, then place in a bowl, cover with a cloth and leave to rest for 30–60 minutes.

3. Knead dough for 2–3 minutes. Divide into 6 balls of equal size, then flatten each ball a circle, about 12 1/2 cm in diameter.

4. Heat an ungreased griddle or electric frying pan until hot. Place one chapati at a time on hot surface. As soon as bubbles appear on surface of chapati, turn the chapati over. Press down on chapati with a thick cloth so that it cooks evenly.

5. To finish chapati, lift it with a fish slice and hold it carefully over an open gas flame without turning until it puffs up slightly. Alternatively, place the chapati under a hot grill.

6. Repeat with remaining dough circles. Keep cooked chapatis hot in a covered napkin-lined basket.

Makes 15

# PITTA BREAD

## Ingredients

385mL warm water
1 teaspoon caster sugar
1 tablespoon dried yeast
500g strong plain flour
1/2 teaspoon salt
oil for greasing

## Method

1. Pour half of the warm water into a jug. Stir in sugar and dried yeast. Set aside in a warm place for 10 minutes until frothy.

2. Sift flour and salt into a bowl. Add yeast liquid and enough of remaining warm water to make a firm but pliable dough. Knead on a lightly floured surface for 10 minutes until dough is smooth and free from cracks.

3. Form dough into a ball, place in a greased bowl, cover with cling film and leave to stand in a warm place for 1 1/2 hours or until dough has doubled in bulk.

4. Turn dough onto a lightly floured surface and knead for 2–3 minutes, then divide into 8 equal pieces, shaping each piece into a ball. Place on greased baking sheets, cover and leave to prove in a warm place until well risen and spongy. Preheat oven to 230°C.

5. Place two dough balls on each baking sheet, flatten slightly and brush with a little cold water. Bake for 10 minutes. Cool on wire racks.

Makes 8

## SIMPLE PILAU RICE

### Ingredients

400g basmati rice, rinsed

6 cloves

5cm cinnamon stick, crushed

6 green cardamom pods, crushed

$1/2$ teaspoon ground turmeric

55g raisins

30g slivered almonds

2 bay leaves

1 tablespoon sugar

salt

7 tablespoons melted ghee or oil

$1/2$ teaspoon cumin seeds

1 tablespoon fresh root ginger, grated

### Method

1. Soak rice in cold water for 10 minutes. Drain and spread on a clean cloth to dry.

2. Transfer rice to a platter. Sprinkle over whole cloves, a few pieces of cinnamon stick, the cardamoms, turmeric, raisins, almonds, bay leaves, sugar and salt.

3. Drizzle over half a teaspoon of melted ghee or oil. Using your hand, mix spices thoroughly into rice. Leave for 15 minutes.

4. Heat remaining ghee or oil in a large saucepan. Add cumin seeds, ginger and rice mixture. Fry gently for 5 minutes until rice is transparent.

5. Add hot water to cover rice by 1cm. Bring to the boil, lower heat and simmer until all liquid is absorbed and rice is tender. Before serving, turn rice over gently.

Serves 4–6

# vegetables

# Crunchy, crisp colourful CONTRASTS

All Indians, young and old, seem to adore vegetables, often preferring them to meat, fish or poultry. A walk through a big, bustling food bazaar is a total sensory experience. It is a riot of brilliant colour and abundance. Market-goers bargain for gleaming, smooth-skinned eggplants, tomatoes and chillis, rough-textured potatoes, carrots, turnips, creamy cauliflowers and green vegaetables of every hue in the form of beans, peas, okra, cabbages, spinach, zucchinis, cucumbers and lettuce ... all spilling from humble stalls onto pavements where other vendors sit selling their produce.

The key to the popularity of vegetables in India is that, whether exotic or familiar, they are prepared in so many innovative and appetising ways. India can easily claim to be the world's leader in vegetable and vegetarian cooking.

Millions of Indians are vegetarians, especially in the south including strict Hindus. A devout Buddhist will not even crack an egg. Vegetables are cooked in a little liquid, which is not discarded and never boiled, so that nutrients are retained. This cooking method is known as wet cooking. Dry cooking is when the vegetables are sliced or shredded and stir-fried with whole spices.

In the South, cauliflower, potatoes, peas, onions and chillies are cooked in a mildly spiced creamy, coconut sauce in the south. In Kashmir, spiced spinach, onions and mushrooms with cream is a wonderful stir-fried main served with lamb, stuffed bread and rice. Spinach is superb as are peas when cooked with paneer (home-made cheese).

Try our exciting salads at home, but be wary of salads when travelling in India as the water in which the ingredients are washed may be unsafe.

## GREEN BEAN SALAD WITH CORIANDER AND GINGER

### Ingredients

700g fresh snake beans
2cm piece fresh ginger
1 tablespoon vegetable oil
1 tablespoon sesame oil
1 teaspoon mustard seeds
2 teaspoons ground cumin
$1/2$ teaspoon turmeric
1 fresh green chilli, finely minced
145mL chicken or vegetable stock
juice of 2 lemons
1 bunch fresh coriander leaves, washed, dried then chopped
salt to taste
85g peanuts, roasted and chopped and lemon wedges to serve

### Method

1. Trim beans to lengths of 8cm and discard any discoloured ends. Peel ginger and cut into fine matchstick-sized pieces.

2. In a wok, heat vegetable and sesame oils and, when hot, add mustard seeds. Allow to cook for a moment or two until seeds start popping. Add ginger and cook for a further minute. Add cumin, turmeric and chilli and stir until fragrant about 2 minutes.

3. Add beans and toss in flavoured oil to coat beans thoroughly. Add stock, simmer for 5–8 minutes or until liquid has almost evaporated completely, and beans are tender.

4. Remove lid and add lemon juice, coriander and salt. Stir thoroughly to combine all ingredients then cool. Serve garnished with roasted chopped peanuts and, lemon wedges, if desired.

Serves 4

## INDIAN CHICKPEA SALAD WITH SPINACH

### Ingredients

2 cups dried chickpeas

4 onions

1 teaspoon whole cloves

4 bay leaves

60mL peanut or olive oil

4 cloves garlic

1 teaspoon turmeric

2 teaspoons cumin

2 teaspoons garam masala

3 tablespoons tomato paste

2 red capsicums, sliced

4 medium zucchinis, sliced on the diagonal

salt and pepper, to taste

2 bunches of spinach or 500g baby spinach

### Method

1. Pick over chickpeas and remove any that are discoloured. Place all remaining chickpeas in a large saucepan and cover with cold water. Peel 2 onions and chop in half. Place in saucepan with chickpeas. Add cloves and bay leaves bring to boil and simmer for 10 minutes. Remove chickpeas from heat and cover and allow to steep for 2 hours. Strain chickpeas, keeping the water.

2. Chop the remaining 2 onions. Heat oil and sauté the onions and minced garlic. Add all spices and cook briefly to release fragrance. Add chickpeas and 2 cups of the soaking water, tomato paste and the capsicum.

3. Cover and simmer gently for about 20 minutes until chickpeas soften and liquid evaporates. Add zucchini and salt and pepper and stir well. Remove from heat. Allow to cool slightly then fold through spinach leaves. Cool completely and serve.

Serves 8

## CAULIFLOWER AND PEAS IN CHILLI SAUCE

### Ingredients

2 tablespoons oil

1 teaspoon mustard seeds

1/2 teaspoon hot chilli powder

pinch of asafoetida

1 cauliflower, divided into florets

125g fresh or frozen peas (thawed if frozen)

1 potato, cut into 1cm cubes

2 tomatoes, peeled and finely chopped

1/2 teaspoon ground turmeric

1/2 teaspoon aadoo mirch
   spice mix (page 14)

pinch of salt

1 tablespoon chopped fresh coriander leaves

1 teaspoon molasses

400mL water

### Method

1. Heat oil in a heavy-based saucepan over moderately high heat. Add mustard seeds. As soon as seeds pop, stir in chilli powder and asafoetida. Shake pan briefly over heat, then add cauliflower florets and peas.

2. Fry, stirring, for a few seconds, then add potato cubes, tomatoes, turmeric, aadoo mirch, salt, coriander and molasses.

3. Stir well, cover and cook for 3–4 minutes, then add the water, mixing thoroughly. Lower heat, cover and simmer for about 30 minutes or until vegetables are tender and sauce has thickened slightly. Serve hot with kadak puri or chapatis (see page 40).

Serves 4

## MOGUL SALAD

(below)

### Ingredients

200g mung bean sprouts

3 cucumbers, diced

4 teaspoons grated fresh or
   desiccated coconut

2 tomatoes, diced

1/4 bunch fresh coriander leaves, chopped

1/2 bunch fresh mint leaves, chopped

1/2 bunch fresh basil leaves, chopped

1 bunch spring onions, chopped

2 tablespoons lemon juice

salt and freshly ground black pepper

### Method

1. Place bean sprouts, cucumbers, coconut,
   tomatoes, coriander, mint and basil leaves,
   spring onions, lemon juice, and salt and black
   pepper in a bowl and toss to combine.
   Cover and stand at room temperature for
   2–3 hours before serving.

Serves 6

## ONION BHAJIS

### Ingredients

250g gram or wholemeal flour

1 tablespoon salt

1 teaspoon garam masala (page 14)

2 tablespoons fresh mint leaves, chopped

1 teaspoon fresh coriander leaves, chopped

4 onions, thinly sliced

oil for deep-frying

### Method

1. Sift flour, salt and garam masala into a bowl. Add
   enough water to make a stiff batter.

2. Stir in mint, coriander and onions, mixing well.

3. Heat oil for deep-frying. Scoop up about a
   tablespoon of mixture at a time and use a
   second spoon to mould it into a roughly round
   shape. Drop into hot oil. Cook for 3 minutes,
   then remove with slotted spoon. You can cook
   several bhajis at once but take care not to crowd
   the pan.

4. When oil has heated up again return bhajis to
   pan for 2–3 minutes more or until dark brown
   and crisp. Drain on paper towels before serving.

Serves 4

## VEGETABLE KORMA

### Ingredients

2 tablespoons vegetable oil

2 tablespoons green masala curry paste (page 14)

1 teaspoon chilli powder

1 tablespoon fresh ginger, finely grated

2 cloves garlic, crushed

1 onion, chopped

500g cauliflower, cut into florets

200g green beans

3 baby eggplants

2 carrots, sliced

125g button mushrooms

400g canned tomatoes mashed in their juices

1 cup vegetable stock

### Method

1. Heat oil in a saucepan over medium heat, stir in masala paste and chilli powder and cook for 2 minutes. Add ginger, garlic and onion and cook, stirring, for 3 minutes or until onion is soft. Add cauliflower, beans, eggplants, carrots and mushrooms and cook, stirring, for 5 minutes.

2. Stir in tomatoes and stock, and bring to the boil. Reduce heat and simmer, stirring occasionally, for 20 minutes or until vegetables are tender.

Serves 4

## POTATO AND PEA BHAJIS

### Ingredients

3–4 tablespoons oil

1 onion, thinly sliced

1 teaspoon ground turmeric

1 teaspoon cumin seeds

1/4 teaspoon ground ginger

1 green chilli, seeded and chopped

500g potatoes, peeled and diced

250g fresh or frozen peas (thawed if frozen)

chopped fresh coriander leaves to garnish

### Method

1. Heat oil in a flameproof casserole, add onion and fry for 5–7 minutes, stirring frequently, until browned but not crisp.

2. Stir in turmeric, cumin seeds, ginger and chilli, then add potatoes and cook gently for 5 minutes, stirring frequently.

3. Stir in peas. Cover casserole and simmer over very low heat for 15–20 minutes or until potatoes are tender but retain their shape. Garnish with coriander and serve.

Serves 4

## SPICED PEAS AND CARROTS

### Ingredients

250g frozen or fresh peas

2 carrots, diced

2 tablespoons vegetable oil

1 teaspoon cumin seeds

2 teaspoons fresh ginger, finely chopped

2 fresh red or green chillies,
  finely chopped

5–6 tablespoons water

salt to taste

*Dry spice mixture:*

1/2 teaspoon ground cumin

1/4 teaspoon ground coriander

1/4 teaspoon mango powder

1/4 teaspoon ground turmeric

### Method

1. For spice mixture, place cumin, coriander, mango powder and turmeric in a small bowl. Mix to combine and set aside.

2. Boil or microwave peas and carrots, separately, until just cooked. Drain, refresh under cold running water and set aside. Heat oil in a heavy-based saucepan over low heat, add cumin seeds, ginger and chillies, and cook, stirring, for 2–3 minutes. Add peas and carrots and mix to combine well. Stir in water and salt and simmer for 5 minutes. Add spice mixture and simmer, stirring occasionally, for 5 minutes longer.

*To microwave:* Place peas, carrots, oil, cumin seeds, ginger, chillies and spice mixture in a microwave-safe dish. Cover and cook on medium, stirring occasionally, for 20 minutes. Season to taste with salt.

Serves 4

# poultry & meat

# Marvellous for a MAHARAJAH

Hindus don't eat beef because for them, the cow is sacred. Some Hindus don't eat any meat in company with vegetarian Buddhists. Muslims and Jews are forbidden to eat pork. Some Muslims and Jews are so strict that they will not eat if they believe the pot or pan has been previously used to cook pork. But the remaining Indian population who enjoy, and can afford, lamb, beef, pork, goat and chicken (which is especially popular during festivals) make the most of them.

Meat markets in India are eye-openers as conditions can not be described as hygienic. People buying poultry choose live birds from cages. Chicken is less expensive, more available, and therefore more popular than duck.

The tandoori and rich biryani dishes to follow hail from the north whose cuisinewas influenced by the conquering Moghuls and Muslims. Northern dishes are relatively mild. The meat, chicken and other ingredients in these dishes are cooked in ghee. The further south one travels, the hotter the food becomes with added quantities of chilli. Southern food tends to be cooked in oil. Christian Goans have perfected cooking pork. Most dishes containing cashews come from Goa which produces these nuts plentifully.

You may be tempted to use commercial curry powders or pre-mixed curry sauces to flavour your poultry or meat instead of the individual spices generally recommended. But by using the latter, you can vary quantities – less chilli or more coriander – to suit the tastes of family and friends. You can also interchange meats: use beef instead of lamb for the korma or lamb instead of chicken in Kashmiri chicken. Chicken rogan josh can easily become lamb or beef rogan josh. Just alter the cooking times accordingly; poultry takes less time to cook than other meats.

## TANDOORI CHICKEN

### Ingredients

2 x 1 kg fresh chickens

3 tablespoons tandoori spice mix (see page 14)

200g tub natural yoghurt

2 tablespoons lemon juice

2 tablespoons melted butter

lettuce leaves, onion rings, tomato wedges
  and lemon for serving

### Method

1. Rinse chickens inside and out and pat dry with paper towels. Make deep gashes in thighs and on each side of breast. Pin back wings.

2. Mix tandoori spice mix, yoghurt, lemon juice and melted butter together. Place chickens in a stainless steel or other non-metal dish and spread mixture all over, rubbing well into gashes. Preheat oven to 190°C. Cover and refrigerate for 12 or more hours. Place chickens on a roasting rack in a baking dish and spoon any remaining marinade over chickens.

3. Place in preheated oven and cook for 1 hour. Baste with pan juices during cooking. When cooked, cover with foil and rest for 10 minutes before serving.

4. Arrange crisp lettuce leaves on a large platter and cover with onion rings. Cut chicken into portions and place on the platter. Garnish with tomato wedges and lemon slices and serve immediately.

Serves 4–6

## LAMB KORMA

### Ingredients

1 1/2 kg shoulder of lamb
salt and freshly ground black pepper
2 tablespoons ghee (page 40)
1 red onion, finely chopped
1 clove garlic, finely chopped
1 tablespoon green masala curry paste (page 14)
1/4 teaspoon ground ginger
1/4 teaspoon turmeric
1/8 teaspoon cayenne pepper
2 tablespoons flour
1 1/4 cups chicken stock
3/4 cup sultanas
145mL yoghurt
1 tablespoon lemon juice
rice and sambals to serve

### Method

1. Cut lamb from bone and chop into 4cm cubes. Season with salt and pepper.

2. Heat ghee in a large, heavy-based saucepan, add one third of the lamb and brown well on all sides. Remove and brown remainder in 2 batches.

3. Add onion and garlic and sauté until transparent. Stir in curry paste, spices and flour and cook for 1 minute. Add chicken stock, sultanas and lamb. Cover with a lid and simmer gently for 1 hour or until lamb is very tender. Stir occasionally during cooking.

4. Stir in yoghurt and lemon juice. Serve with boiled rice and sambals.

Serves 4–6

## CHICKEN BIRYANI

(opposite, top)

### Ingredients

3 tablespoons ghee

3 onions, sliced

1 1/2 kg chicken pieces

2 teaspoons fresh ginger, grated

3 cloves garlic, crushed

1/2 teaspoon ground cumin

1/2 teaspoon ground cinnamon

1/4 teaspoon ground cloves

1/4 teaspoon ground cardamom

1/4 teaspoon ground nutmeg

1/2 teaspoon flour

1 cup chicken stock

1/2 cup natural yoghurt

1/2 cup cream

*Rice pilau:*

2 tablespoons ghee

1/2 teaspoon ground saffron

1/2 teaspoon ground cardamom

1 teaspoon salt

200g basmati rice, well washed

4 cups chicken stock

2 tablespoons sultanas

### Method

1. Heat ghee in a large frying pan and cook onions for 2–3 minutes or until golden brown. Remove from pan and set aside.

2. Add chicken to the pan and cook until well browned on all sides. Remove from pan and set aside.

3. Combine ginger, garlic, cumin, cinnamon, cloves, cardamom, nutmeg and flour. Stir into pan and cook for 1–2 minutes. Add stock, yoghurt and cream, stirring to lift pan sediment.

4. Return chicken to pan with half the onions. Cover and simmer for 15–20 minutes. Remove from heat and let stand, covered, for 15 minutes.

5. To make rice pilau, heat ghee in a large saucepan. Cook saffron, cardamom, salt and rice for 1–2 minutes. Pour in stock and bring to the boil. Add sultanas, reduce heat and cook gently for 10–15 minutes or until most of stock is absorbed. Cover and set aside for 10 minutes. Preheat oven to 180°C.

6. Transfer half the rice to a large ovenproof dish, top with chicken pieces, then remaining rice. Drizzle over sauce from chicken, top with remaining onions and cashew nuts. Cover and bake for 20–30 minutes.

Serves 4

## MUSTARD CHILLI PORK

(opposite, bottom)

### Ingredients

750g pork fillets

55g melted butter

30g ghee

2 tablespoons peanut oil

3 onions, chopped

1 tablespoon black mustard seeds

2 cloves garlic, crushed

2 red chillies, chopped

1/2 teaspoon ground cumin

1/2 teaspoon ground turmeric

1 tablespoon brown sugar

1 cup water

1 tablespoon lime juice

8 lime leaves

### Method

1. Trim meat of all visible fat, brush with melted butter and bake at 180°C for 25–30 minutes.

2. Heat ghee and oil in a saucepan, cook onions, mustard seeds, garlic and chillies for 2–3 minutes or until onions soften.

3. Stir in cumin, turmeric, brown sugar, water, lime juice and lime leaves. Bring to the boil, then reduce heat and simmer, uncovered, for 10 minutes or until mixture reduces and thickens.

4. Transfer mixture to a food processor or blender. Process until smooth, then return to pan. Slice pork diagonally and add to mustard mixture. Heat through gently and serve.

Serves 4

*chicken biryani*

*mustard chilli pork*

## TANDOORI LAMB CUTLETS

(below)

**Ingredients**

8 lamb cutlets

*Marinade:*

4 tablespoons natural yoghurt

1 teaspoon fresh ginger, grated

1 clove garlic, crushed

1 tablespoon lime juice

1 teaspoon ground cumin

$1/4$ teaspoon ground cardamom

$1/4$ teaspoon chilli powder

$1/4$ teaspoon garam masala

few drops red food colouring

**Method**

1. Trim meat of all visible fat and set aside.

2. To make marinade, combine yoghurt, ginger, garlic, lime juice, cumin, cardamom, chilli powder and garam masala. Add red food colouring until marinade is pink. Add cutlets, toss to coat and set aside to marinate for 30 minutes.

3. Remove cutlets from marinade. Grill or barbecue for 6–8 minutes, turning and basting with marinade frequently.

Serves 4

## KASHMIRI CHICKEN

**Ingredients**

1 onion, finely chopped

3 tablespoons fresh root ginger, grated

2 cloves garlic, crushed

$1/2$ teaspoon ground coriander

$1^1/2$ teaspoon anchovy essence

1 cup almonds or cashew nuts, ground

1 tablespoon oil

4 chicken portions, skinned

1 cup chicken stock

1 cup thick coconut milk

2 teaspoons light brown sugar

**Method**

1. Mix onion, ginger, garlic, coriander and anchovy essence with ground almonds or cashews to form a paste.

2. Heat oil in a large heavy-based saucepan. Add paste and stir over moderate heat for 5 minutes.

3. Add chicken portions and cook for 15 minutes, stirring frequently to coat in spice mixture and seal.

4. Pour in stock, stirring to incorporate spice mixture. Bring to the boil, lower heat and simmer for 20 minutes.

5. Stir in coconut milk and brown sugar, turn heat to lowest setting and simmer for 20 minutes more. Serve hot.

Serves 4

## CASHEW NUT BUTTER CHICKEN

### Ingredients

55g ghee or butter

2 cloves garlic, crushed

2 onions, minced

1 tablespoon Madras curry paste (page 14)

1 tablespoon ground coriander

1/2 teaspoon ground nutmeg

750g boneless chicken thigh or breast
   fillets, cut into 2cm cubes

55g cashew nuts, roasted and ground

1 1/4 cups double cream

2 tablespoons coconut milk

### Method

1. Melt ghee or butter in a saucepan over medium heat, add garlic and onions and cook, stirring, for 3 minutes or until onions are golden.

2. Stir in curry paste, coriander and nutmeg and cook for 2 minutes or until fragrant.

3. Add chicken and cook, stirring, for 5 minutes or until chicken is brown.

4. Add cashews, cream and coconut milk, bring to simmering and simmer, stirring occasionally, for 40 minutes or until chicken is tender.

*Note:* To roast cashews, spread nuts over a baking tray and bake at 180°C for 5–10 minutes or until lightly and evenly browned. Toss back and forth occasionally with a spoon to ensure even browning. Alternatively, place nuts under a medium grill and cook, tossing back and forth until roasted.

Serves 6

## INDIAN SALAD OF SPICED CHICKEN AND DHAL

### Ingredients

6 cups vegetable stock

1 1/2 cups dried lentils

juice of 2 lemons

40mL vegetable oil

1 tablespoon madras curry paste (page 15)

1 tablespoon garam masala

1 teaspoon turmeric

salt and pepper, to taste

4 large chicken breast fillets, skin removed

1 1/2 cups vegetable stock, extra

1 small cauliflower, cut into florets

1 1/2 cups fresh or frozen peas

2 small tomatoes, seeded and diced

1 cucumber, peeled and diced

2 spring onions, sliced

2 tablespoons fresh mint, chopped

2 large bunches watercress, trimmed

fresh mint, extra, for garnish

spring onion for garnish

### Method

1. Bring 6 cups of vegetable stock to the boil and add lentils. Simmer until lentils are tender (about 20 minutes). Drain well then transfer lentils to a large bowl and add lemon juice and 1 tablespoon of oil. Mix well, cover and chill.

2. Combine curry paste, garam masala and turmeric in a plastic bag with salt and pepper then add chicken breasts to bag. Seal bag and shake vigorously. Heat a grill pan or non-stick frying pan with remaining oil until smoking. Then add chicken breasts to pan and fry until golden brown and cooked through on both sides (about 5 minutes). Remove chicken and set aside.

3. To the used pan, add extra 1 1/2 cups of stock and bring to the boil. Add cauliflower and peas and cook over high heat until vegetables are crisp-tender and most of liquid has evaporated, (about 5 minutes). Add vegetable mixture to lentils and mix well. Add tomatoes, cucumber, spring onions and fresh mint and mix well, adding salt and pepper to taste.

4. Slice chicken into diagonal strips then gently mix into salad. Arrange watercress on a platter and top with salad mixture, arranging so that there is plenty of chicken visible. Garnish with fresh mint and spring onion.

Serves 4

## INDIAN MEATBALLS IN TOMATO SAUCE

### Ingredients

500g minced lamb

5 tablespoons natural yoghurt

5cm piece fresh root ginger, finely chopped

1 green chilli, deseeded and finely chopped

3 tablespoons fresh coriander leaves, chopped

2 teaspoons ground cumin

2 teaspoons ground coriander

salt and black pepper

2 tablespoons vegetable oil

1 onion, chopped

2 cloves garlic, chopped

1/2 teaspoon turmeric

1 teaspoon garam masala

400g can chopped tomatoes

### Method

1. Mix together lamb, 1 tablespoon of yoghurt, ginger, chilli, 2 tablespoons of coriander, cumin and ground coriander and season with salt and pepper. Shape the mixture into 16 meatballs.

2. Heat 1 tablespoon of oil in a large saucepan, then fry meatballs for 10 minutes, turning until browned. You may have to cook them in batches. Drain on kitchen towels and set aside.

3. Heat remaining oil in pan. Add onion and garlic and fry for 5 minutes or until softened, stirring occasionally. Mix turmeric and garam masala with 1 tablespoon of water, then add to onion and garlic. Add remaining yoghurt, 1 tablespoon at a time, stirring well each time.

4. Add tomatoes, meatballs and 150mL of water to mixture, and bring to the boil. Partly cover pan, reduce heat and simmer for 30 minutes, stirring occasionally. Sprinkle rest of the coriander leaves over to garnish.

Serves 4

## ROASTED TANDOORI CHICKEN BREASTS

### Ingredients

4 skinless and boneless chicken breasts

*Marinade:*

1 teaspoon salt

2 cloves garlic, chopped

2¹/₂ cm piece fresh root ginger, chopped

1 tablespoon fresh coriander leaves, chopped plus extra leaves to garnish

1 tablespoon fresh mint, chopped

¹/₂ teaspoon turmeric

¹/₂ teaspoon hot chilli powder

2 cardamom pods, husks discarded and seeds reserved

4 tablespoons natural yoghurt

juice of ¹/₂ lemon

### Method

1. For marinade, grind salt, garlic, ginger, coriander, mint, turmeric, chilli powder and cardamom seeds to a paste, using a mortar and pestle or coffee grinder kept especially for that purpose. Transfer to a large, non-metallic bowl, stir in the yoghurt and lemon juice and mix together well.

2. Score each chicken breast 4 times with a sharp knife, then add to bowl and turn to coat thoroughly. Cover and chill for 6 hours, or overnight.

3. Preheat oven to 220°C. Place chicken breasts on a rack in a roasting tin and cook for 20–25 minutes until tender and until the juices run clear when pierced with a skewer. Serve with salad and naan bread (page 37).

Serves 4

## LAMB AND SPINACH CURRY

### Ingredients

2 tablespoons vegetable oil

2 onions, chopped

2 cloves garlic, chopped

2¹/₂ cm piece fresh root ginger,
   finely chopped

1 cinnamon stick

¹/₄ teaspoon cloves, ground

3 cardamom pods

600g diced lamb

1 tablespoon ground cumin

1 tablespoon ground coriander

4 tablespoons natural yoghurt

2 tablespoons tomato paste

1 cup beef stock

salt and black pepper, to taste

500g fresh spinach, finely chopped

2 tablespoons roasted flaked almonds

### Method

1. Heat oil in a flameproof casserole dish or large heavy-based saucepan. Fry onions, garlic, ginger, cinnamon, cloves and cardamom for 5 minutes to soften onions and garlic, and to release flavour of the spices.

2. Add lamb and fry for 5 minutes, turning, until it begins to colour. Mix in cumin and coriander, then add yoghurt, 1 tablespoon at a time, stirring well each time.

3. Mix together tomato paste and stock and add to the lamb. Season with salt and pepper. Bring to the boil, then reduce heat. Cover and simmer for 30 minutes or until lamb is tender.

4. Stir in spinach, cover and simmer for another 15 minutes or until mixture has reduced. Remove cinnamon stick and cardamom pods and mix in almonds. Serve with steamed rice.

Serves 4

## PORK VINDALOO

### Ingredients

3 small dried red chillies

1 teaspoon cumin seeds

1½ teaspoon coriander seeds

2 cloves

4–6 black peppercorns

2½ cm cinnamon stick

2½ cm piece of fresh root ginger, grated

2 cloves garlic, chopped

3 tablespoons vinegar

500g lean pork, cubed

pinch of salt

3 tablespoons oil

2 onions, finely chopped

red chillies to garnish

water

### Method

1. Dry-fry chillies, cumin seeds, coriander seeds, cloves, peppercorns and cinnamon stick in a frying pan for a few minutes, until mixture starts to crackle. Do not let it burn.

2. Using a mortar and pestle, or a coffee grinder kept especially for the purpose, grind spices along with ginger, garlic and vinegar to a smooth paste.

3. Place pork cubes in a saucepan with salt. Pour in water to cover meat by about 2½ cm. Bring to the boil, lower heat and simmer for 45 minutes or until meat is tender.

4. Meanwhile heat oil in a large frying-pan. Fry onions for about 10 minutes, until golden. Stir in spice paste and fry for 2 minutes more, stirring constantly.

5. Drain meat, reserving cooking liquid, and add it to frying-pan. Stir well, cover and cook for 10 minutes over moderate heat.

6. Add about 2 cups of reserved cooking liquid. Stir well, cover and cook for 15–20 minutes more, or until meat is coated in a thick spicy sauce.

7. Serve at once, garnished with red chillies, or tip into a casserole, cool quickly, and refrigerate for reheating next day.

Serves 4

## CHICKEN ROGAN JOSH

### Ingredients

8 skinless boneless chicken thighs

1 tablespoon vegetable oil

1 small red capsicum and 1 small green capsicum, deseeded and thinly sliced

1 onion, thinly sliced

5cm piece of fresh root ginger, finely chopped

2 cloves garlic, crushed

2 tablespoons garam masala

1 teaspoon of each paprika, turmeric and chilli powder

4 cardamom pods, crushed

salt

200g Greek yoghurt

400g chopped tomatoes

fresh coriander to garnish

### Method

1. Cut each chicken thigh into 4 pieces. Heat oil in a large heavy-based frying pan and add capsicums, onion, ginger, garlic, spices and a good pinch of salt. Fry over low heat for 5 minutes or until capsicums and onion have softened.

2. Add chicken and 2 tablespoons of yoghurt. Increase heat to medium and cook for 4 minutes or until yoghurt is absorbed. Repeat with rest of yoghurt.

3. Increase heat to high, stir in tomatoes and 200mL of water and bring to the boil.

4. Reduce heat, cover, and simmer for 30 minutes or until chicken is tender. Stir occasionally and add more water if sauce becomes too dry.

5. Uncover pan, increase heat to high and cook, stirring constantly, for 5 minutes or until sauce thickens. Garnish with coriander.

Serves 4

## LAMB PILAU WITH YOGHURT

### Ingredients

500g lean boneless leg lamb, cubed

6 cloves

8 black peppercorns

4 green cardamom pods

1 teaspoon cumin seeds

2¹/₂ cm cinnamon stick

1 tablespoon coriander seeds

2 small red chillies

5 cups water

2 tablespoons ghee or oil

1 onion, finely chopped

2 tablespoons fresh root ginger, grated

2 cloves garlic, crushed

500g basmati rice, soaked for
    30 minutes in enough water to cover

¹/₂ teaspoon salt

lemon to garnish

yoghurt to serve

### Method

1. Put lamb cubes in a saucepan. Tie cloves, peppercorns, cardamom pods, cumin seeds, cinnamon, coriander seeds and chillies in a muslin bag and add to pan with the water.

2. Bring to the boil, lower heat and simmer for 40 minutes or until meat is very tender. Strain, reserving lamb cubes and stock but discarding spice bag.

3. Heat ghee or oil in a large frying pan, add onion, ginger and garlic and fry for 2 minutes, stirring frequently.

4. Add lamb cubes, stirring to coat them in spices. Cook for 10 minutes until golden brown.

5. Meanwhile drain rice and transfer to a large saucepan. Pour in enough reserved stock to cover rice by about 4cm. Add salt. Bring to the boil, cover, lower heat and cook for 10–15 minutes or until rice is almost tender and most stock has been absorbed.

6. Add rice to meat mixture in pan; fork through lightly. Cover tightly and cook over very low heat until rice is tender, adding more stock if necessary. Garnish with lemon and serve with yoghurt.

Serves 4–6

## MADRAS CURRY

### Ingredients

30g plain flour

salt and freshly ground black pepper to taste

500g stewing steak, cubed

55g ghee or 4 tablespoons oil

2 onions, finely chopped

1 teaspoon ground turmeric

1 teaspoon ground coriander

1 teaspoon cayenne pepper

1/2 teaspoon ground black mustard seeds

1/2 teaspoon ground cumin

2 cloves garlic, crushed

145mL hot water

55g seedless raisins

### Method

1. Place flour in a stout polythene bag and season with salt and pepper. Add stewing steak, close bag and shake until evenly coated.

2. Heat ghee or oil in a heavy-based pan, add floured beef cubes and fry for 5 minutes, stirring and turning meat so that all sides are browned.

3. Add onions and cook, stirring occasionally, for 5 minutes longer.

4. Stir in spices and cook for 3 minutes, then add garlic. Cook for 2 minutes.

5. Add the hot water. Bring to the boil and boil briskly, stirring constantly, for 5 minutes.

6. Stir in raisins and add more water, if necessary, to cover meat. Bring to the boil, lower heat and simmer for 2 1/4 hours, adding more water as required. Serve at once or cool swiftly, refrigerate and reheat next day.

Serves 4

## MASALA DUCK CURRY

### Ingredients

1 tablespoon sesame oil

2 kg duck, cleaned and cut into 8 pieces

1 onion, chopped

2 small fresh red chillies, finely chopped

1 stalk fresh lemongrass, finely chopped
   or ¹/₂ teaspoon dried lemongrass, soaked
   in hot water until soft

2 tablespoons green masala
   curry paste (see page 15)

1¹/₂ cups coconut milk

3 fresh or dried curry leaves

1 tablespoon lime juice

1 tablespoon brown sugar

1 tablespoon fresh coriander leaves, chopped

30g fresh basil leaves

3 fresh green chillies, seeded and sliced

2 fresh red chillies, seeded and sliced

### Method

1. Heat oil in a saucepan over medium heat. Add duck and cook, turning frequently, for 10 minutes or until brown on all sides. Remove and drain on absorbent kitchen paper.

2. Add onion, chopped red chillies and lemongrass to pan and cook, stirring, for 3 minutes or until onion is golden. Stir in masala paste and cook for 2 minutes longer or until fragrant.

4. Stir in coconut milk, curry leaves, lime juice and sugar and return duck to pan. Bring to boil and simmer, stirring occasionally, for 45 minutes.

5. Add coriander, basil and sliced green and red chillies and cook for 10 minutes longer or until duck is tender.

Serves 4

# seafood

# Curry flavour
# WITH A CATCH

Fishing is a major industry in India. The men harvest at sea while the women await the landing of the distinctive, often colourful boats. In many communities it is the women who sort and grade the catch and scurry to the bazaar with loaded baskets to sell.

On the west coast, the people of tropical Goa and Kerala frequently use coconut, from the palms which line their splendid beaches, to add an aromatic delicacy to their fish curries. The Parsis, who mostly settled north on the same coast at former Bombay, enjoy sweet and sour flavours, and have influenced seafood preparation in Maharashtra state. Equally famed for its seafood is the east-coast state of West Bengal, of which Calcutta is the capital. A Bengali meal without fish is rare indeed. Flavours are pungent, with an emphasis on mustard paste, chillies and tamarind. Fish is often baked in banana leaves, a method also favoured in Mumbai. Lobster and prawns are also favourites in this region.

## TIKKA SKEWERS

### Ingredients

750g firm white fish fillets, cut into
  2cm wide strips
1 lemon, cut into wedges

*Spicy yoghurt marinade:*
1 onion, chopped
4 cloves garlic, crushed
2 teaspoons fresh ginger, finely grated
1 tablespoon ground cumin
1 tablespoon garam masala
3 cardamom pods, crushed
1 teaspoon ground turmeric
2 teaspoons chilli powder
2 teaspoons ground coriander
1 tablespoon tomato paste
1 3/4 cups natural yoghurt

*Cucumber raita:*
1 cucumber, finely chopped
1 tablespoon fresh mint leaves, chopped
1 cup natural yoghurt

### Method

1. Pierce fish strips several times with a fork and place in a shallow glass or ceramic dish.

2. To make marinade, place onion, garlic, ginger, cumin, garam masala, cardamom, turmeric, chilli powder, coriander and tomato paste in a food processor or blender and process until smooth. Add yoghurt and mix to combine. Spoon marinade over fish, toss to combine, cover and marinate in refrigerator for 3 hours.

3. Preheat barbecue to medium heat. Drain fish and thread onto lightly oiled skewers. Place skewers on lightly oiled barbecue grill and cook, turning several times, for 5–6 minutes or until fish is cooked.

4. To make raita, place cucumber, mint and yoghurt in a bowl and mix to combine. Serve skewers with lemon wedges and raita.

**Note:** When buying fish fillets look for those that are shiny and firm with a pleasant smell of the sea. Avoid those that are dull, soft, discoloured or oozing water when touched.

Serves 6

## GOAN-STYLE FISH AND COCONUT CURRY

### Ingredients

2 tomatoes

2 cardamom pods, husks discarded
  and seeds reserved

1 teaspoon each of ground coriander,
  cumin, cinnamon and hot chilli powder

1/2 teaspoon ground turmeric

2 tablespoons water

2 tablespoons vegetable oil

1 onion, finely chopped

1 clove garlic, finely chopped

2 1/2 cm piece fresh root ginger,
  finely chopped

400mL can coconut milk

680g skinless white fish fillet, such as haddock
  or cod, cut into 2 1/2 cm chunks

salt, to taste

fresh coriander to garnish

### Method

1. Place tomatoes in a bowl, cover with boiling water and leave to stand for 30 seconds. Peel, then finely dice flesh.

2. Crush cardamom seeds using a mortar and pestle. Add coriander, cumin, cinnamon, chilli powder, turmeric and water and mix to a paste. Set aside.

3. Heat oil in a large, heavy-based saucepan. Fry onion, garlic and ginger for 3 minutes or until softened. Add spice paste, mix well and fry for 1 minute, stirring constantly.

4. Pour in coconut milk and bring to the boil, stirring. Reduce heat and simmer for 10 minutes or until liquid has reduced slightly. Add fish, tomatoes and salt. Partly cover pan and simmer, stirring occasionally, for a further 10 minutes or until fish turns opaque and is cooked through. Garnish with coriander to serve.

Serves 4

## BAKED FISH

### Ingredients

2 large onions, roughly chopped

1 tablespoon vegetable oil

2 cloves garlic, crushed

2 fresh red or green chillies,
   finely chopped

2 teaspoons fresh ginger, finely chopped

1 tablespoon cumin seeds

2 bay leaves

salt to taste

4 large tomatoes, finely chopped

1/2 teaspoon ground cumin

1/2 teaspoon ground coriander

pinch of ground cloves

pinch of ground cinnamon

pinch of ground cardamom

1/2 teaspoon mango powder

1/4 teaspoon ground turmeric

3 tablespoons double cream

4 firm white fish fillets, such as
   John Dory or ocean perch

1 bunch fresh basil leaves, finely chopped

### Method

1. Place onions in a food processor or blender and process to make a purée.

2. Heat oil in a heavy-based saucepan, add garlic, chillies, ginger, cumin seeds, bay leaves, salt and onion purée. Cook over a medium heat until onions are a pinkish colour. Add tomatoes, cumin, coriander, cloves, cinnamon, cardamom, mango powder and turmeric and cook, stirring, for 3–4 minutes. Remove pan from heat and stir in cream.

3. Preheat oven to 180°C. Place fish in a baking dish, pour sauce over and bake for 20 minutes or until fish flakes when tested with a fork. Just prior to serving, sprinkle with basil.

Serves 4

# SPICY RED PRAWNS

## Ingredients

16 large uncooked prawns, shelled
    and deveined
3 large tomatoes, peeled, seeded
    and chopped
1 tablespoon vegetable oil
1 small bunch coriander leaves, chopped

### Marinade:

6 cloves garlic, finely chopped
2 teaspoons fresh ginger, finely chopped
8 fresh red or green chillies,
    finely chopped
3 tablespoons lemon juice
1 tablespoon caster sugar
salt to taste

## Method

1. To make marinade, place garlic, ginger, chillies, lemon juice, sugar and salt in a bowl and mix to combine. Add prawns and toss to coat with marinade. Cover and marinate in refrigerator for 15–24 hours.

2. Place tomatoes in a food processor or blender and process until smooth.

3. Preheat oven to 160°C.

4. Heat oil in a wok or large frying-pan, reduce heat and add prawns with marinade and cook, stirring constantly, for 2–3 minutes.

5. Transfer all to a casserole dish and add the tomatoes and coriander then mix well tom combine.

6. Cover and bake in oven for 30 minutes. Serve in casserole dish with side bowls of boiled rice.

Serves 4

## CHILLI SESAME PRAWN KEBABS

### Ingredients

1 tablespoon vegetable oil

1 tablespoon madras curry paste (see page 15)

2 tablespoons fresh ginger, finely grated

2 cloves garlic, crushed

2 tablespoons lime juice

1/2 cup natural yoghurt

36 uncooked medium prawns,
    shelled and deveined, tails left on

6 tablespoons sesame seeds, toasted

*Green masala onions:*

30g ghee or butter

2 onions, cut into wedges

2 tablespoons green masala
    curry paste (see page 15)

### Method

1. Place oil, madras curry paste, ginger, garlic, lime juice and yoghurt in a bowl and mix to combine. Add prawns and toss to coat. Cover and marinate in the refrigerator for 2–3 hours.

2. Drain prawns and thread 3 prawns onto an oiled skewer. Repeat with remaining prawns to make 12 kebabs. Toss kebabs in sesame seeds and cook on a lightly oiled, preheated medium barbecue or under a grill for 3 minutes on each side or until prawns are cooked.

3. To make masala onions, melt ghee or butter in a saucepan over a medium heat. Add onions and cook, stirring, for 5 minutes or until soft. Stir in green masala paste and cook for 2 minutes longer or until heated through. Serve with the kebabs.

Serves 6

# desserts

# Golden to
# SILVER TASTES

Indian dessert is usually not served with a family meal. At special festival times and celebrations, such as weddings, Indians indulge their passion for sweet, very sweet foods.

Indian desserts seem unusual to many Westerners. Rice pudding comes in exotic guises. The West has long been acquainted with various nuts and some aromatic spices such as powdered cardamom, cloves, saffron, cinnamon, nutmeg, ginger, vanilla essence and coconut, but not in the combinations used on the sub-continent. In one recipe, green peas form the basis of the dessert!

Milk and yoghurt are used extensively in Indian sweets. Real silver leaves, beaten until paper thin and edible, are surprising ingredients available at some specialty stores selling Indian fare.

Ice cream is rarely served in Indian homes but our mango ice cream makes an appropriate, light finish to a rich dinner. It can also be made with drained, crushed pineapple intead of mango and garnished with mint.

Other Indian desserts include small balls of cream cheese served in rosewater and caster sugar syrup or balls mixed with almonds, cardamom and a little sweetened condensed milk. And, believe it or not, fritters of banana, pineapple, pear or apple are also common, as they are all over Asia. Fritters distinctively Indian, flavour your usual sweet batter mix with cardamom and cinnamon, cut all fruits into big cubes and cook in batches. You can serve each guest little fritters of each fruit, white with sifted icing sugar and drizzled with rosewater-flavoured syrup.

## INDIAN RICE PUDDING WITH PISTACHIOS

### Ingredients
55g basmati rice
2 cups full-fat milk
400g full-cream evaporated milk
butter for greasing
3 cardamom pods, husks discarded and seeds reserved
1 cinnamon stick
55g caster sugar
2 tablespoons flaked almonds roasted
30g shelled pistachios, roughly chopped

### Method
1. Preheat oven to 150°C. Place rice, milk and evaporated milk in a small, heavy-based saucepan and bring to a simmer, taking care not to let mixture boil. Simmer, uncovered, for 10 minutes.

2. Butter an ovenproof dish. Transfer rice mixture to dish, then stir in cardamom seeds, cinnamon stick, sugar, almonds and pistachios, reserving 1 tablespoon pistachios to garnish. Bake for 2 hours, or until reduced to a thick consistency, stirring in the skin that will form on top every 30 minutes. Remove cinnamon stick. Serve warm or cold, garnished with reserved pistachios.

Serves 4

## ORANGE CARDAMOM CAKES

### Ingredients

2 cups of plain flour

1 1/2 teaspoons baking powder

1 teaspoon bicarbanate of soda

2 teaspoons ground cardamom

1/2 cup butter, softened

1 cup sugar

zest and juice of 2 oranges

2 large eggs

2/3 cup yoghurt

3 tablespoons marmalade

2 tablespoons boiling water

2 tablespoons sugar, extra

*Orange sauce:*

2 cups sugar

1 cup water

juice of two oranges

2 tablespoons thick cream

4 large oranges, peeled and segmented

### Method

1. Preheat oven to 180°C and generously grease twelve 1 cup capacity non-stick muffin tins.

2. In a large bowl, combine flour, baking powder, baking soda and ground cardamom. Set aside.

3. Using an electric mixer, cream butter, sugar and orange zest together until light and fluffy. Add eggs and yoghurt and mix on low speed until ingredients are well combined, then fold flour mixture by hand. Do not over-mix.

4. Divide batter evenly among the 10–12 muffin tins and bake for 15–18 minutes. Meanwhile, whisk together fresh orange juice, marmalade, boiling water and extra 2 tablespoons sugar.

5. When orange cakes are ready (test with a skewer), remove muffin tins from the oven and spoon orange syrup over cakes. Allow to cool in the tins.

6. Meanwhile, make sauce. Mix together sugar and water and stir until sugar has dissolved. Raise heat and boil vigorously, washing down sides of pan with a pastry brush dipped in cold water. Continue boiling until syrup turns a rich, deep gold then remove pan from heat. Carefully add orange juice to syrup (be careful because it will splatter). Swirl pan to dissolve juice, returning pan to heat if necessary. Once mixture is smooth, remove from heat and set aside to cool. When cool, whisk in the cream then chill.

7. To serve, turn out cakes and place each on a plate. Heap orange segments on top of cakes. then spoon sauce all around.

Serves 6–8

## ALMOND BARFI

### Ingredients

250g blanched almonds

145mL milk

125g sugar

145mL water

400g condensed milk

170g butter, diced

### Decoration:

silver leaf (optional)

55g pistachio nuts, shelled
   and roughly chopped

### Method

1. Grease a 25 x 20cm baking tin. Grind almonds with a little of the milk in a blender or food processor to make a rough paste. Add remaining milk and blend briefly.

2. Put sugar and water in a heavy-based saucepan. Stir over gentle heat until sugar has dissolved. Increase heat and boil rapidly until mixture registers 115°C on a sugar thermometer, the 'soft ball' stage..

3. Stir almond paste and condensed milk into syrup. Add butter and stir until fully dissolved.

4. Bring mixture to the boil again and boil until it again registers 115°C.

5. Pour barfi mixture into prepared tin; spread evenly. Carefully lay silver leaf on top, if using, then sprinkle with pistachio nuts. Cool, then refrigerate overnight to set.

6. Allow barfi to return to room temperature before cutting into squares or diamonds to serve.

Makes about 30 pieces

## MANGO ICE CREAM

### Ingredients

2 x 400g cans sliced
  mangoes, drained
4 tablespoons lemon juice
170g superfine sugar
2 eggs, separated
300mL double cream, whipped
strawberries for garnish (optional)

### Method

1. Set aside a few mango slices for decoration. Purée mango with lemon juice and caster sugar in a blender or food processor. Transfer to a bowl. Cover and refrigerate.

2. Using an electric mixer, beat egg yolks until pale and creamy. In a separate bowl, beat egg whites until stiff.

3. Fold egg yolks into cream, then fold in mango purée. Finally, fold in stiffly beaten egg whites.

4. Spoon mixture into an ice-cream maker and chill according to instructions. Alternatively, freeze in ice cube trays. When semi-frozen, beat mixture to break up any large ice crystals. Repeat the process once more, then freeze in a suitable container until solid.

5. Soften slightly before serving. Decorate with strawberries and the reserved mango slices.

Makes approx. 4 cups

## GULAB JAMUN

### Ingredients

170g sugar

2¹/₂ cups water

8 green cardamom pods

30g self-raising flour

125g powdered skimmed milk

30g ghee or butter

30g cream cheese

1–2 tablespoons rosewater

2–3 tablespoons milk or natural
   low fat yoghurt

oil for deep-frying

### Method

1. Put 155g of the sugar with the water in a wide saucepan or deep frying-pan. Stir over gentle heat until sugar has dissolved, then add cardamom pods. Increase heat and boil for 15 minutes to make a light syrup. Reduce heat to lowest setting to keep syrup warm.

2. Combine flour and powdered milk in a bowl. Rub in ghee or butter, then add remaining sugar, cream cheese, rosewater and enough milk or yoghurt to form a soft dough. Knead lightly and roll into 18 small balls (jamuns).

3. Heat oil for deep-frying. Cook jamuns in small batches, keeping them moving in the oil until they are golden brown all over.

4. When golden brown, remove *jamuns* with a slotted spoon and drain on paper towels for 5 minutes. Remove syrup from heat and carefully add *jamuns*. Allow to cool to room temperature in syrup. To serve, transfer *jamuns* to individual plates with a slotted spoon, then add 2–3 tablespoons syrup.

*Note:* These small dumplings in a spicy syrup are a traditional dessert. They are usually made with full-fat powdered milk. This is not always easy to obtain, so this recipe uses skimmed milk powder and adds cream cheese.

Serves 6

## JALLEBI

### Ingredients

*Batter:*

500g plain flour

1/2 teaspoon salt

1 cup natural low-fat yoghurt

2 teaspoons sugar

2 tablespoons easy-blend dried yeast

oil for deep-frying

*Syrup:*

500g soft light brown sugar

1 litre water

1 cinnamon stick, broken into short lengths

8 green cardamom pods

4–6 cloves

### Method

1. Sift flour and salt into a large bowl, make a well in the centre and add yoghurt. Stir, gradually incorporating surrounding flour to make a smooth batter. Stir in sugar and yeast, cover and set aside in a warm place for 4–6 hours until batter is well risen.

2. To make syrup, put sugar and water in a heavy-bottomed saucepan. Stir over gentle heat until sugar has dissolved, then add cinnamon, cardamom pods and cloves. Increase heat and boil rapidly until syrup is thick and heavy and has reduced by half. Reduce heat to lowest setting to keep syrup warm while cooking jallebi.

3. Heat oil for deep-frying. Fill a large piping bag, fitted with a narrow nozzle, with jallebi batter. Squeeze batter in spirals into hot oil, stopping the flow when each jallebi measures about 10cm across. (Do not cook too many jallebi at the same time. Remove with a slotted spoon as soon as they are golden brown.)

4. Drain jallebi on paper towels, then dip into pan of hot syrup. Dip for up to 5 minutes, depending on how sweet you like your jallebi. Drain off excess syrup and serve.

*Note:* Jallebi are deep-fried spirals of cooked sweet batter which are dunked – or soaked – in a sweet spicy syrup.

Makes about 20

# INDEX